Raising

| **G** | RATED |

Kids in an

| **R** | RATED WORLD |

Raising G RATED Kids in an R RATED WORLD

WRITTEN BY JOHN CALDWELL

Pleasant Word
A Division of WINEPRESS PUBLISHING

Pleasant Word (a division of WinePress Publishing, PO Box 428, Enumclaw, WA 98022) functions only as book publisher. As such, the ultimate design, content, editorial accuracy, and views expressed or implied in this work are those of the author.

ISBN 13: 978-1-4141-0781-3
ISBN 10: 1-4141-0781-1
Library of Congress Catalog Card Number: 2006905774

Dedication

Dedicated to
JACK AND WILL
whose lives bring so much joy to Granny and PawPaw

Table of Contents

Introduction   ix

1. Show Affection   13
2. Learn to Communicate   21
3. Spend Time   33
4. Have Fun   45
5. Provide Discipline   57
6. Teach Values   75
7. Set Boundaries   91
8. Control the Media   101
9. Deal with Substance Abuse   115
10. Lead Them to Christ   127
11. Respond to Rebellion   141
12. Ascribe Value   151

Endnotes   163

Introduction

I started preaching the summer after my first year in Bible College. The people at Louisburg Christian Church in Missouri were very kind, tolerant, and patient with me; and the four years I spent there were certainly some of the best years of my life. I dated and married Jan while I served there. I was ordained into the Christian ministry, finished college, conducted my first weddings and funerals, and learned a lot about life, all while I ministered to that congregation.

I also preached some great sermons on parenting while I was at Louisburg. We didn't have a lot of young families in that rural congregation; but that didn't matter. Some of my sermons probably weren't all that relevant. But I really excelled when it came to telling people how to raise their kids. When I first went to Louisburg I wasn't even married. And it was only after leaving the ministry there that our first child was born. But I could easily tell those people how to raise their kids because I didn't have any experience to contradict my theories.

Our son, Shan, was born our first year of traveling in full-time evangelistic work. His sister, Jennifer, came along five years later, just after we began what was to be our more than 30-year ministry with Kingsway Christian Church. For many years I fell rather silent on the subject of parenting. My theories were a work in progress. It was only as our kids got older and appeared to be doing all right that I felt the freedom to once again speak out on the subject; but even then it was not with the same sense of certainty I had exhibited as an unmarried, childless, young preacher.

Now our children are grown, married, and have lives of their own, quite independent of any control on our part. We are now enjoying the reward of not killing our kids, that of being grandparents. And while we have no illusions about our kids being perfect, (at least I don't, although Jan says, "They are practically perfect in every way"), they both love the Lord with all their hearts, have spouses who are devoted believers, are actively involved in their respective churches, and model the values that I believe are pleasing to Christ. They are serving Him in their respective professions, Shan as a pastor and Jennifer as a physical therapist. In most every way they are making their parents very proud. Thus I not only feel the freedom but also some sense of obligation to write this book.

Both Paul and Peter address the need for older Christians to instruct younger Christians out of their experience. (See 1 Tim., Titus, and 1 Pet.) Unfortunately, the church as a whole has not done a good job of follow-ing that teaching. Sometimes younger Christians have not respected or sought out the advice of those who are older in the faith; and many of us who are older in the faith have been reluctant, for whatever reason, to share the understanding we have gained in the school of experience.

Personally, I dislike the whole concept of armchair experts—those who can tell others how to do what they've never done. There was some benefit in my early attempts at preaching on parenting. First, I exposed the people to both biblical principles and to my very limited, but still valid, observations of the parenting skills of others. But the fact remained that I had not done it myself. Many of you have attended the seminars presented by Bill Gothard over the years. And while he certainly taught many valid principles and helped many people, there was an inherent weakness because he was teaching as an unmarried, non-parent. You say, "Jesus was an unmarried, non-parent." Yes, but Jesus was and is the Son of God. And even at that, you don't find a lot in the gospels about parenting, except in the example of our Heavenly Father.

I like having good role models myself. I heard my friend, Glen Liston, deliver a great sermon on the family during a large, national convention. Later, another friend criticized his sermon as not being realistic because he had presented the family as what it should be—a mother and father strongly committed in love to each other with children instructed in the ways of the Lord and required to submit to the authority of their parents. The critic said Liston should have addressed the broken home and rebellious children, for that was more the norm. But in Christianity, it seems to me we should be holding the bar high and challenging people with things as they ought to be, even while extending grace to those who fall short.

Let me offer this disclaimer. Jan and I are certainly not perfect parents. If we could do it all over again there are a number of things we would do differently. Shan and Jennifer were not and are not perfect kids. As they grew older, I did begin to use family illustrations, always and only with their permission. Although many people expressed appreciation, I also received and still receive much criticism. Individuals have said, "I'm tired of hearing about your perfect kids." Just recently a lady had asked my wife for her input regarding a parenting issue, and when Jan responded, the woman said sarcastically, "Well, my children weren't born perfect like yours." Again, we have no illusions about being perfect parents, but our children have turned out well, and we're very proud of them.

Let me also offer the disclaimer that the fact that our children have turned out well is not simply due to our doing the right things as parents. Much of the good in our children's lives is simply due to the grace of God. Indeed, we have all known parents who did "everything right" whose kids really messed up. And we have all known of kids who were raised in horrible circumstances who have turned out wonderfully. But Jan and I know we have done some things right, and that's the focus of this book. Hopefully, we've also learned from some of our mistakes, and it is our desire that you benefit from our mistakes.

You may not yet be a parent but want to get a head start. You may feel as if you are a parenting failure, perhaps the parent of preschoolers who are driving you nuts. You may have elementary aged children and don't feel as if you can even reason with them. Perhaps your child is an adolescent and your home resembles a war zone. Or it could be that your children are grown and you're not even sure they know where you live or remember your phone number. Maybe you don't even have biological children but you carry the responsibility of knowing you are a role model for the children of others.

I believe the principles covered in this book are transferable and that, with the help of the Holy Spirit, they can be customized to fit your situation.

There is one more point I want to make before we get to work. God intends for your children to bring joy to your life. Parenthood is a remarkable gift of God's grace. Look at Ps. 127:3-5:

> Children are a gift from the Lord; they are a reward from Him. Children born to a young man are like sharp arrows in a warrior's hands. How happy is the man whose quiver is full of them! He will not be put to shame when he confronts his accusers in the city gates.

Clearly, children are intended as a blessing to be enjoyed, not a hardship to be suffered. But having children also makes you very vulnerable. Years ago I wrote down this quote, which I've certainly found to be true: "Making the decision to have a child—it's momentous. It is to decide forever to have your heart go walking around outside your body."

Chapter One

Show Affection

Let me offer another disclaimer right from the beginning. There is no methodology that guarantees "G-Rated" (Great Kids) in an "R-Rated" (Rotten World). This book is about doing the right thing, which, in turn, increases the likelihood of your kids turning out right. And we parents have to measure our success in parenting by the degree to which we follow God's design for parenting and not necessarily by how our kids turn out. We do live in a fallen world, and eventually our children do become sinners. They can exercise free will to do what is right or that which is wrong, even *very* wrong.

Christians invariably point to Prov. 22:6 (NLT) as their guarantee: "Teach your children to choose the right path, and when they are older, they will remain upon it." Many people take this to say that if you give your kids a good, positive home, if you teach them and discipline them, if you take them to church and Sunday school, and if you get them to read the Bible and be involved in the youth program, they will turn out to be godly, responsible, Christian adults. However, that is not what that verse says. The King James and New American Standard translations', "Train up a child in the way he should go…" is even more prone to misunderstanding. And many parents believe if they raise their children right, even if their kids do go astray for a while, by the time they are old, they will return to the "right path."

As a general rule, parents who follow God's parenting guidelines will more often end up with godly kids. The statistics demonstrate that children who grow up in Christ-honoring homes are far more likely to remain faithful to Christ than those who grow up in homes that dishonor Christ. But Prov. 22:6 is first of all a truism, not a promise. There are many such truisms in Scripture, especially in Proverbs. For instance, Prov. 22:4 reads, "True humility and fear of the Lord leads to riches, honor, and a long life." But we certainly don't take that to be an absolute promise that if you are humble and fear the Lord you are going to get rich and live a long time.

Secondly, the meaning of Prov. 22:6 has more to do with helping children become their own unique selves, helping each child find the way *he or she* should go, the right path *he or she* should follow. This verse teaches that if we work to develop our children's uniqueness, they won't depart from what God intended them to be later in life, but will instead be fulfilled. Too many parents try to force their agendas on their children instead of training their children up in the way they should go—the way God uniquely designed them. We all know of dads who have tried to force sons into athletics who were more disposed to intellectual pursuits or mothers who forced piano lessons on a daughter who had no interest in music whatsoever. Often the intent is to vicariously fulfill the desires of the parent rather than training up a child in the way "…he should go."

The bottom line is that there are no guarantees. Some kids are going to break your heart no matter what you do. But doing the right things greatly increases the likelihood of your children growing into parent-honoring, responsible, Christ-loving adults. And to me that begins with showing affection and unconditional love for our children. We're going to come back to the "unconditional" part later. But I want to start with the very practical area of showing or demonstrating affection or love. While there are areas in which I know Jan and I have been deficient, I want to start here partly because it's one area in which I feel we've done well. Although there are many ways to express affection, without a doubt there are three that are by far the most meaningful: talk, touch, and time.

TALK

Many parents, especially dads, feel that their children should know that they love them just because they provide for them. But affection must be verbalized. From the time we first held our children, we've told them we love them. Our children never went through one day of their lives while living at home without being told they were loved multiple times. Still to this day, every time we see them, every time we talk to them on the phone, every time we leave, "I love you" is part of the conversation. Even when our grandson, Jack, was only two years old, he would close every phone conversation with "Luv, Paw-Paw."

Neither Jan nor I grew up in outwardly expressive homes. Oh, we both knew we were loved. But neither set of parents was expressive about it. My mother died at ninety-four, and although I know she loved me with all her heart, it was only in the last couple of decades of her life that she learned to say, "I love you," each time we talked. I point this out for two reasons. First, you may be saying that you simply aren't an expressive person; but you can learn to be. Secondly, I point this out as a reminder of the fact that there are many children out there who are hungry for words of affection. If they don't hear those words at home, they'll go seeking them elsewhere

Jerry Johnston tells of one girl whose teen years were filled with partying, drugs, alcohol, and having sex with one guy after another if he said, "I love you," only to figure out on her own that her promiscuous life had come out of her thinking that her mother and dad didn't love her enough to tell her. She found a Kleenex on which was the clear imprint of her mother's lips and she carefully folded it and carried it with her. And when she got terribly lonely, she would take out her mother's Kleenex and press her mother's lip print upon her cheek.[1] Who knows just how many children and teens are just that desperate for expressions of affection.

Proverbs 18:21 reminds us, "…the tongue can kill or nourish life." Gary D. Chapman says that the words, "I love you" are like a gentle rain falling on the soul of a child, while harsh cutting words spoken out of short-lived frustration can damage a child's self esteem and be remembered for a lifetime."[2] Tell your kids you love them. You can't do it too often.

Despite all the emphasis on nonverbal communication, verbalizing your love and affection is still indispensable. And be careful of the words you use to express affection. Sometimes what we mean to be affectionate can be destructive. Nowhere is this more obvious than in the use of nicknames. You may mean "Twerp, Dweeb, Geek, or Shorty" to be affectionate, but "Princess, Champ, Hero, Sunshine, and Beautiful" are affectionate and positive at the same time. Someone once said, "I was almost nine before I learned that my name wasn't 'Shut Up!'"

I mentioned that I wasn't raised in a family that was expressive about affection. As a matter of fact, I can only remember my dad verbalizing his affection one time. I was in high school. I was riding with him in his 1960 Chevrolet station wagon. We were on our way up Highway 13 to the family farm. I could take you to the exact curve in the road today, where my dad reached over, put his big, calloused hand on my neck, and said, "I love you, son." Talk to your kids. Tell them you love them.

TOUCH

We are all at least somewhat aware of the importance of physical touch in expressing affection. Even little babies need to be picked up, cuddled, and spoken to. Long before a child understands the concept of love he or she will feel loved through a loving, physical touch. Physical touch includes hugs and kisses, but also includes a pat on the back, a high-five, holding hands, or just a touch on the shoulder. Shan's boys experience his touch as they play wrestle on the floor. I read somewhere that a child needs a minimum of eight hugs a day just to stay healthy and they need twelve to fifteen if you really want them to prosper. Well, I doubt that hugging can be reduced to a mathematical formula, but physical touch is a powerful communicator of affection and love.

We've always been a hugging family. We used to do—still do occasionally—a family hug. Charlie, our lovable beagle hound, always was jealous and forced his way into the middle of the group hug. Even dogs need affection. But we are also a family that shows that kids are very different. Shan always wanted hugs more than Jennifer; but that doesn't mean that Jennifer didn't need them just as much or more.

Part of that may go back to Shan's preschool days. We were traveling in evangelistic work and pulled a travel trailer, which was our home away from home. Our bedroom was in the back and Shan slept on a couch up front. Invariably he would show up at our bedside sometime in the predawn hours, blankie in hand, wanting to get in bed with us. Jan would say, "You can get in bed with us when God turns the lights on." Sure enough, he'd be back at the crack of dawn and settle in between us. During the day he would have his mother's undivided attention. One of my most enjoyable mind pictures is of Shan curled up on his mother's lap, watching Captain Kangaroo on our tiny little TV.

Shan was a hugger and kisser even through his high school days. Until he was old enough to have his own car we would often drop him off for school—our kids hated the school bus. He would invariably lean over and give me a hug and a kiss on the cheek. As a teenager, Jennifer was much more concerned about what others thought so she wasn't nearly as demonstrative. However, I still got my hug. Actually Jennifer's favorite thing was having her back scratched and also curling up with her mom while watching TV.

By the way, as important as loving touch is on a regular basis, there are times when it is even more important. Times like immediately after corrective discipline or a conflict; times of grief after losing a contest, competition, being hurt by a friend, or having a major disappointment; and times of joy such as reaching a goal, winning a victory, receiving an award, or solving a difficult problem. When it is most difficult, it is most important.

So don't back off on touching your children. Daughters especially need their fathers to continue to touch them appropriately, even after or especially after they have gone through puberty and are maturing physically. When a father treats his daughter differently after she has reached adolescence, it sends a message that either something is wrong with her or she is no longer loved as she once was. Many teenage girls feel rejected when their daddies stop hugging on them and touching them appropriately. Study after study has shown a direct connection between promiscuity and lack of physical touch from fathers. If girls are not touched appropriately by their dads, they will very likely seek that acceptance and touch from other males in inappropriate ways.

A daughter's first attempts to reach across the sex barrier to please men will be with her own father. She needs to know she is acceptable to him, that she's attractive, and that she's intelligent. If she is affirmed by him she will see her value as a person, not as a sex object. So dads, keep telling your daughters you love them, but keep hugging too. And moms, your sons may resist and say, "Aw, mom!" but they need it too.

You will not always be in physical proximity to your children so as to touch them physically. But I want you to know that there are many nonphysical ways to reach out and touch your kids as well. Jan has always done a great job with this. When our kids went away to college, she wrote to them at least once a week even though we talked on the phone. When Jennifer was in college 500 miles away and could rarely come home, there were flowers sent on special occasions. From the time our kids were little Jan would fix them special birthday cakes. I can still remember Shan's first birthday. We were in a revival in Rogers, Ohio. But Jan borrowed someone's kitchen to make him a rocking horse birthday cake. And to this day, wherever we go—and we love to travel—Jan sends the kids post cards reaching out with hugs across the miles.

When we become touchers and huggers we are following the greatest example we can follow, for touch was such an important part of the life of Jesus. He touched the blind, the lame, the deaf, and the diseased. He touched the brokenhearted and the downtrodden. But most of all, Jesus touched the children. Read again Mark 9:36-37, "Then [Jesus] put a little child among them. Taking the child by the arms, he said to them, 'Anyone who welcomes a little child like this on my behalf welcomes me, and anyone who welcomes me welcomes my Father who sent me.'"

The importance of touch simply cannot be overemphasized. A study of newborns revealed that after ten days, infants who were massaged for 45 minutes a day gained 47 percent more weight than those not regularly touched. In a study of the elderly it was discovered that nursing home patients who received regular, meaningful touch increased food intake, increased weight, and decreased erratic behavior.[3] Everyone needs touch. Especially your kids!

TIME

The third way to express affection is through the dedication of time. When you carve time out of your busy schedule just to be with your kids it shouts out love to them. When your children come to you with something that's important to them and you put down the newspaper or put the TV on mute and take the time to listen, it communicates volumes to them about how much you care about them. A lack of time also communicates volumes—but not in a positive way. And here are the sad facts: a California study revealed that the average father of pre-schoolers spends 37 seconds a day actively involved with his children; and a Maryland study said that the average parent spends 15 minutes a week in meaningful dialogue with their children.[4]

One of the best ways to express affection for our children is by giving them time, quality time, and our undivided attention. When your children are small it may mean reading *Horton Hears a Who* for the thousandth time or tickle wresting on the floor or going to the playground to play. It may later be walks in the woods where you and your child just look, listen, and talk. But the main thing to remember is to spend that quality time primarily doing things they want to do. What joy you can bring to the heart of a small child by getting down on the floor and playing with Tonka trucks, a Fisher-Price airport, or a Barbie cruise ship. Older kids will love that time spent at the amusement park, the zoo, or just getting ice cream. A trip to the mall or a concert by a group of their liking—not necessarily yours—will communicate love and affection like you can't believe.

How well do you know your kids? Have you met their best friends? Could you name their best friends? Do you know their favorite athletes, TV programs, or movie stars? Do you know your children's hopes and dreams? Could you tell me what they have on the walls of their rooms? Without quality time, all those things will remain unanswered questions, and the biggest question of all will be, "Do Dad and Mom really love me or do they just tolerate me?" Gary Chapman quotes eight-year old Bethany who said, "I know my Dad loves me. He took me fishing last week. I don't know if I like fishing, but I like being with my daddy."

This point is so important that we are going to devote an entire chapter to the issue of time. Time, talk, and touch, they're the big three of expressing affection. That's not to say there aren't other ways. Giving gifts, acts of kindness and thoughtfulness, meaningful family traditions, standing up for your kids, all have a part in expressing affection. Inside family jokes and games provide a loving atmosphere.

Years ago, J. Alan Peterson did a weekend seminar in our church where he told of something he did with his daughter that I adapted for mine. I would go up to Jennifer, put my arms around her, and say, "Jennifer, you're beautiful, you're wonderful, I love you, I'm so lucky to have you for my daughter…" and she would break away and run screaming out of the room. But I know, and she knows that I know, that she loved every minute of it.

Few, if any, things are more important in raising "G-Rated Kids" than providing affection and expressing it in ways that leave no doubt in their minds that they are loved unconditionally. A child who knows he or she is loved has the self-confidence to excel at being himself or herself. But a child, uncertain of his or her parents' love will often seek it in negative ways. Look for ways this week to express your affection for your children through talk, touch, and time.

Chapter Two

Learn to Communicate

We began our study of raising "G-Rated" kids by talking about ways to show affection. Love and affection should be the basis of any parent-child relationship. However, I believe with all my heart that good communication is the primary key to every interpersonal relationship. Over the years I've counseled hundreds of couples who are struggling in their marriages. And while the presenting problem—that is what the couple believes to be the problem—may vary greatly, when you dig just below the surface it is easy to determine that had there been better communication the presenting problem would most likely not have arisen. The problem appeared to be finances, but had the couple communicated well they wouldn't have gotten in financial trouble. The problem appeared to be a strained relationship with the in-laws, but had the couple really talked through the issues they would never have gotten to that point of alienation.

I tell every couple with whom I do premarital counseling that the number one problem in marriage relationships is poor communication. Good communication is so important that a popular magazine polled over 30 thousand women and found they agreed that poor communication was their number one problem. Most said that if they had it to do all over again they would choose a husband who had the ability to communicate.

The same thing is true in parenting. If there is good communication, many of the issues that impact our children negatively can be avoided. Let me go so far as to say that parenting is largely communication. And in this world where our kids are receiving good, bad, and terrible communication from the world, it is important that we parents be in a position to help our kids sort that out. They get a lot of conflicting messages. A coach might be telling your son he's a wonderful athlete while his math teacher is telling him he is a terrible student while the girl of his dreams is telling him he's a loser by shooting him down. Is there any way you can even know that all of that is going on, let alone reinforce the positive messages he needs to hear?

When your children are small, you have much more control over what is being communicated to them. But unless bridges of communication are built early on, it will be difficult to be there for them in a meaningful way in those teen years when the usual thing is for communication to shut down anyway. Good communication from an early age can bind a family together for the challenges that are sure to come. The word *communicate* comes from the same root word as community and communion. Communication—at least good communication—brings us together and strengthens our relationships. Through communication we share information, and in the case of a family, we share intimacy and identity as well. By the way, good parent-child communication facilitates good communication by your children with God.

Fortunately, there are ways to encourage good communication in your parent-child relationships. I want to give you four major keys that are certainly helpful in raising "G-Rated" kids that will also help you maintain your sanity during your child-rearing days.

Jan and I are very fortunate that our kids talked to us about almost everything. When they came in from a date they came into our bedroom, sat on the end of our bed, and told us about their evening. I remember Jennifer calling us on the phone from a school dance to tell us about her first real kiss. On our father-daughter dates during her teen years we talked about everything from French-kissing to the physical assets of the latest girl Shan was dating. As a high school senior she was criticized by a Bible college student she had dated for telling her parents too much. She quickly set him straight saying, "There is nothing going on in my life that I want to keep from my parents." Shan was not quite so open, but as boys go, we had great communication as well.

KEY NUMBER ONE: MAKE OPPORTUNITIES FOR COMMUNICATION

There will be certain recurring themes in this book and one of them has to do with making time for your kids and spending time with your kids. Some of the best opportunities for communication are unplanned and spontaneous but occur simply because you are together. It begins early on with doing things like reading to your infants and toddlers.

I must have read every Dr. Seuss book written at least a hundred times to each of our kids; now I'm starting over with our grandkids. Also, spend lots of time playing with them when they're little. Among other things, you are building a special relationship that will greatly facilitate communication, as they grow older.

Jan worked for a Christian organization when we were first married while I finished college. But we are very fortunate that we were able to choose for Jan to be a stay-at-home mom. Therefore, she always invested a tremendous amount of time in our kids. From kindergarten on, she was there for them when they got home from school. As a matter of fact, she often picked them up from school. At home they would lie on the bed and debrief on the activities of the day. That process lasted from kindergarten all the way through high school.

When possible I picked the kids up from school. When I had to run errands, I always asked one of the kids to ride along. Some of the best communication took place in those entirely unstructured, non-threatening times of just being together doing routine things. Of course, there were planned times as well. I'll write more later about weekly date nights with my daughter and nights out with my son, one-on-one times that were not only bonding times but times to talk about anything and everything that was on their minds or mine. To this day I take trips with my married daughter just for fun, but we also catch up on what's going on in her life. And when we have the chance, Shan and I still go and hit a bucket of balls at the driving range because it provides a relaxing forum in which to interact. No pressure, just opportunity.

I was interested enough in communicating with my daughter that I often took her shopping, even during her teen years. We had such a great relationship during those years that she was agreeable to being seen in public with her dad! You've got to make opportunities for communication.

The issue of time is so significant that I'm going to dedicate an entire chapter to it later in the book. However, the question always arises as to which is more important, quantity time or quality time. Early in my ministry I bought into that whole idea of quality time being what was really important. I spoke critically of those dads who were always there but who were always watching TV or preoccupied with something else and never gave their kids quality time. However, I have long since learned that quality time can't be manufactured or produced on demand. It takes quantity time to produce quality time. Parents whose schedules are so focused on financial gain or career mobility that little time is left to interact with their kids are only fooling themselves if they believe they can pull off meaningful communication.

Those who lived in Bible times were restricted to slow travel and were free of modern-day technology, so they seemed to have naturally experienced more opportunities for interaction with their children than we enjoy today. Moses spoke to that when he wrote in Deut. 6:7: "Repeat them [God's commands] again and again to your children. Talk about them when you are at home and when you are away on a journey, when you are lying down and when you are getting up again."

Modern-day life does not lend itself to casual interaction. Those conversations occurred more naturally in the natural flow of everyday life even a century ago. Today it takes real determination and intentionality to provide such opportunities. But creating those opportunities is Key Number One to developing good parent-child communication.

KEY NUMBER TWO: BECOME AN EFFECTIVE LISTENER

The fast-paced lifestyle of the times we are living in does not encourage good listening. The media screams at us from every side, along with the technological distractions that abound and mitigate against us being effective listeners to anyone, especially to our children. We listen to the boss. We listen to our clients or customers. And our spouses at least try to make sure we are listening to them. But in this world of power positions, our kids are left with no leverage except for their needs. So if we are going to raise "G-Rated" kids we are going to have to intentionally work at being good listeners. How do you do that? I hope you're not offended by the simplicity of my suggestions; for the truth is, they work.

Step 1: Listen with your eyes as well as your ears

Did you know that some communication experts estimate that actual words make up only about seven percent of communication, while body language comprises 55 percent, and tone of voice the other 38 percent? Have you ever had a conversation with someone who wouldn't look you in the eye? They were communicating all right, communicating lack of interest. But they were also failing to pick up on all of your nonverbal communication.

Listening to your children with your eyes as well as your ears not only facilitates good communication, it is in itself communication. It builds self-worth and lets your kids know you value them. Look at your kids when you're talking to each other. Proverbs 15:30 in the NASB says, "Bright eyes gladden the heart." Don't rob yourself of the blessing of seeing your children's eyes "light up."

Step 2: Give your children focused attention

In his book, *How to Really Love Your Child*, Christian child psychologist Ross Campbell explains focused attention:

> What is focused attention? Focused attention is giving a child our full, undivided attention in such a way that he feels without a doubt that he is completely loved. That he is valuable enough in his own right to warrant parents' undistracted watchfulness, appreciation, and uncompromising regard.[1]

Let me add that focused attention means being quiet so that our kids can talk. I've had the privilege of meeting some truly great people in my lifetime. Most of them have one thing in common, the ability to make you feel like you are the most important person in the world to them right then. They draw you out, ask you to speak, and listen attentively. We should do no less for our kids and by listening carefully and repeatedly as we get to know our children. Your kids will talk if you are a good listener.

Step 3: Provide the right setting

I want to reiterate that the best part of communication happens naturally. We've already talked about making opportunities for communication by spending quantity time with our kids so that there will be those moments when meaningful communication takes place spontaneously. But if there is a specific need for communication to take place and you need to facilitate it, you must provide a place that encourages that communication.

What sort of place is that? It is a place that is quiet enough for you to hear, private enough to relieve the fear of eavesdropping, and comfortable enough to encourage communication. It may be a strategically planned trip in the car or a walk in the park. It might be shooting baskets, playing catch, or hitting that bucket of balls. It might simply be a retreat to the bedroom. Chances are you know the sort of place that will work for your child.

I should also point out that while there are situations that are serious enough to demand the involvement of both parents, as a general rule a child is more likely to open up to one parent rather than both at the same time. Be sensitive to this. Frankly, there were some things my kids talked about more comfortably with Jan, but there were other subjects they felt more comfortable talking about with me.

Step 4: Eliminate distractions

Some years back I wrote a book on evangelism, *Top Priority: Building an Evangelistic Church*. Many of the principles in this chapter are similar to the principles of leading someone to Christ. There is a whole section on learning to listen. Furthermore, I stress the idea of eliminating distractions when leading someone to Christ.

I talk about the role of the "silent partner" in eliminating distractions in an evangelistic setting. One's spouse should certainly be just as sensitive to what is going on when you are really communicating with your child, especially your teenager.

Your spouse can intercept phone calls and entertain friends that might distract you during an important opportunity for communication. Of course, getting away from the television or a blaring radio is important as well.

Step 5: Hear them out

Often, parents are so busy thinking of how we are going to respond to our children that we don't really hear what they are saying in the first place. So be patient. Don't be too quick to respond. Proverbs 18:13 says it well, "What a shame, what folly, to give advice before listening to the facts!" When children feel their opinions are respected or that their cause will get a good hearing, they are much more likely to open up to Mom and Dad.

Don't interrupt, and don't contradict your child while he or she is speaking to you. And for goodness sake, don't make fun of what they have to say unless you are certain they are just having fun with you. Children are people too. Hear them out. Create an atmosphere of acceptance by taking them seriously.

Step 6: Reserve judgment

There were certainly times when my children expressed thoughts with which I disagreed, made value judgments that I felt were wrong, and stated facts that were disappointing to me. And I can't say I have always practiced what I am trying to teach. But I know that in such situations the worst thing to do is to quickly judge and condemn. That is perhaps the fastest way to cut off meaningful communication. If children feel their attempts to communicate will result in condemnation, it is almost a certainty that they will not open up.

I'm not suggesting that we withhold the truth from our kids to avoid offending them. I am suggesting that we hear them out, make sure we understand where they're coming from, and then present a reasoned argument rather than a heated or emotional response. In other chapters we'll deal with teaching our children Christian values, refusing to compromise, and disciplining our children when they violate certain principles and values. What I am suggesting now is that we learn to be good listeners. Believe me when I say that I know it is difficult to listen rather than talk or give unsolicited advice or make judgment calls. But we can do it if the wellbeing of our kids requires it. And it does.

I read recently that suicide is now the number two cause of death among teens. As a pastor, I have personally seen the consequences of parents failing to listen while being quick to judge. Fortunately, the result is not always suicide, but it may be an estrangement between parent and child that robs both of a great deal of joy, and that is tragic. Reserving judgment is a component of good listening.

Step 7: Ask open-ended questions

Although the principles discussed in this chapter apply to every age group, most of them are presented in the context of communicating with adolescents. The application to adolescents is even more important in this action step. Parents may have a wonderful, communicative relationship with their child, only to have all communication cease when that child becomes a teenager.

Have you ever had this conversation with your teenager?
Question: "How did things go at school today?"
Answer: "Fine."
Question: "Did anything interesting happen?"
Answer: "Nah!"
Question: "How are you doing in biology?"
Answer: "Okay."
Question: "Have you got anything special going on tonight?"
Answer: "Nope."
Meaningful communication requires sharing information, feelings, and ideas. One-word answers really don't get the job done. So what do you do when your child retreats to monosyllabic responses to your attempts to prompt communication? I make no guarantees that it will work, but the best you can do is ask open-ended, thought questions that simply can't be answered monosyllabically. Don't ask, "Did anything interesting happen at school today?" but "What was the most

interesting thing that happened at school today?" And don't settle for, "Nothing!" Or how about, "If you were the parent and I was the teenager, what things would you change about the way we run our family?" That ought to get things going. Here's another, "If you could have your greatest wishes fulfilled over the next 12 months, how would life be different for you this time next year?" When your kids know you're really interested in their answers to such questions, it can evoke some very meaningful dialog.

Step 8: Empathize with your kids

If we're going to be effective listeners we must put ourselves in our kids' shoes. Child psychologist and Focus on the Family founder James Dobson once said, "The key to raising healthy, responsible children is to be able to get behind the eyes of the child and see what he [or she] sees, think what he [or she] thinks and feel what he [or she] feels. If you know how to do that, then you know how to respond appropriately for him [or her]."[2]

It is not enough to listen to the words. If we're truly going to listen with understanding, we must listen not just to what they say or even what they mean, but we must listen to what they feel. Now that takes real intentionality, effort, and patience. It means taking the time to study your child, the way he or she thinks, the way he or she reacts, the way he or she responds. But it's worth it. That brings us to yet another key.

KEY NUMBER THREE: STOP, LOOK, AND LISTEN FOR SIGNS

Different people express the same feelings in different ways. The same anger that is expressed with loud, angry words by one child may take the form of silent withdrawal by another. The same love that is expressed in verbal affirmation by one child, may be expressed in helpful deeds by another. Therefore, communication doesn't mean just listening and talking. It means recognizing the signs of various emotions in your children.

Our son and daughter were and are very different in the way they express their feelings. But we soon learned the signs. It was obvious when they were angry, although it was expressed in entirely different ways. It was also obvious when they were excited or hurt or pleased. You must learn your children's signs.

What are some of those signs? They may include, but are certainly not limited to, silence, withdrawal, nervous chatter, locked doors, restlessness, lack of appetite, irritability, misbehavior, sullenness, tears, slamming doors, throwing things, giddiness, pensiveness, singing, and a hundred and one other things. But all are signs. The problem is that you have to learn a different "sign language" for each child.

KEY NUMBER FOUR: RESPOND WITH LOVE AND TRUTH

The emphasis of this chapter is listening. But communication is a two-way street. While a parent must do his or her best to be a good listener—focused, patient, tolerant, and empathetic—parents also have an obligation to do as Paul tells us in Eph. 4:15. That is, we are to speak the truth in love. In other words, the truth is neither to be avoided nor used as a club.

Sometimes we have to tell our children, "That is wrong," or even, "You are wrong." There will be times we must say, "I'm very disappointed in you," or "You've made me very sad." But that's looking at the negative side of communication. Speaking the truth in love many times means saying, "You are absolutely right!" "I am so proud of you." "I'm so glad you are my son or daughter." "You did a great job." "I couldn't agree more!"

Paul says in Eph. 4:29, 31-32:

> Don't use foul language or abusive language. Let everything you say be good and helpful, so that your words will be an *encouragement* to those who hear them…Get rid of all bitterness, rage, anger, harsh words, and slander, as well as all types of malicious behavior. Instead be kind to one another, tenderhearted, forgiving one another, just as God through Christ has forgiven you. (emphasis added)

The purpose of communication should be to build up, not merely express frustration, anger, or disappointment. Paul wrote to Timothy to "patiently correct, rebuke, and encourage your people with good teaching" (2 Tim. 4:2). The purpose was for their good. The motive was to be love. And we parents can do no less for our children. When the communication involves correcting or rebuking, the same grace and forgiveness that we have found available in Christ most certainly should be extended to our children. And when the communication involves commendation, thankfulness, or praise, we ought to be our children's biggest cheerleaders.

Communication, it's the key to everything else. We each have our own obstacles to overcome. Jennifer always said that I gave her intimidating looks. Some people in our church feel I do the same to them. Maybe the obstacle is simply a gruff voice, or maybe it's a schedule that doesn't make you very available. There are ways to overcome every obstacle and to let your kids know that not only are you available, but you are anxious to share in their lives. Let them know that what they think makes a difference and that what they think matters to you.

As with many of the things I'll write about in this book, Jan and I haven't always done what we've known to do. We haven't always practiced what I've preached. But communicating with our kids has always been a high priority. Our kids have always known they could talk to us about anything. As a result, we had some very special conversations during their growing-up days. We kept long distance in business during their college days. And to this day, we talk to our kids and their spouses several times a week. As a matter of fact, Shan called just today to talk with me about an important decision he's facing.

I am a wealthy man to have the relationships I have with my kids. And that is due in great part to good communication.

Chapter Three

Spend Time

In the very first chapter, "Show Affection," I wrote of three specific ways we show affection: talk, touch, and time. We've already expanded on talk in Chapter 2, Learn to Communicate. Now we come to the third of the big three. Spending time with and on our kids is so important that I want to devote an entire chapter just to that subject.

Things are busier than ever for both kids and parents. A Louis Harris poll revealed that since 1973 the hours people in America work has actually increased by 20 percent while the number of leisure hours has dropped by 32 percent.[1] So with overcommitted schedules, over-involved kids, and exhausted parents, it takes real determination to invest significant time in our kids. And yet carving out time for our kids is an absolute must.

Study after study has shown that kids who spend both quality and quantity time involved with their parents in talking, family activities, and building family traditions are far less likely to get involved in bad behavior or harmful activities. Children who regularly have the opportunity to hang out with their parents informally find it far easier to open up to their parents about school, friends, challenges, issues, right and wrong, and especially matters of faith. Those discussions don't come out of a ten-minute chat at the end of a busy day.

Kathi Hunter, in a *Christian Parenting Today* article, called "Connect With Your Kids," quotes Dr. Janice Crouse, a respected authority on family issues who explains:

> Kids learn values when they are spoken to respectfully and feel free to ask questions. When we spend time with our children we can be sensitive to the teachable times in their lives. Even while I watched television with my kids, I would ask them leading questions. "Did you see how that man treated his wife? How could he have handled that situation better?" Those discussions helped my children become more discerning and discriminating in what they watched and the activities they participated in growing up.[2]

So it is that *time* is one of the major building blocks of successful parenting; and if you really want to raise "G-Rated" kids, you're going to have to invest a great deal of time in them. That doesn't just happen in today's society. It has to be done intentionally and with a great deal of thought. So let's look at some ways to reinforce the whole idea of spending time with our kids.

MAKE FAMILY TIME A PRIORITY

This starts with setting priorities on your personal calendar. If you have quality family time and give yourself the opportunity to make wonderful memories with your family it will start with you and your spouse sitting down with the calendar and a pen or pencil and making sure it happens. At the beginning of the year I always took my day timer and marked out days off, family birthdays, holidays, and preplanned family vacation time.

Those things always did and still do take precedence over ministry commitments. Believe me when I say that if days off are not off limits and vacation days are not preplanned, there will be all sorts of pressing issues that will infringe on what would otherwise be family time.

For most of my ministry, Thursday has been my day off. It simply works best with my overall schedule. For the most part, the congregation has always respected my personal and family time. But occasionally I've had some pushy parishioner demand to see me on Thursday. Because I mark my days off at the beginning of the year I can honestly say, "I have no time available that day, I'm all scheduled up." I remember one particularly hostile man who told me that I was his pastor and I had an obligation to see him on a certain Thursday evening. I told him I already had an appointment, and he suggested I get the other person to reschedule because what he needed to talk to me about was very important. I assured him it could not be more important than my previously scheduled appointment because I had a date with my daughter. By the way, I offered to meet with him on Friday morning, at the time of his choosing, even as early as 5:00 A.M. However, he declined. Apparently his issue wasn't really all that important.

My family certainly understood if there was a real emergency. There were times I was at the bedside of a critically ill member on my day off or in the home of the bereaved trying to offer comfort. And the truth be told, there have been a disproportionate number of funerals that have fallen on Thursday. But that's not a problem; it just involves reshuffling the schedule. The point is that you have to make family time a priority on your calendar. The challenge increases as the children grow older. Because now you have to plan not just around your calendar, but also around sports team practices and games, school and club activities, and, yes, church youth group activities as well. Sometimes it seems as if you need a Ph.D. in time management just to work it all out. But you must decide as a family that shared experiences are a priority or they will get squeezed out.

So making family time a priority begins with your calendar and schedule. However, it also includes planned activities. Some families set aside one evening a week as family night. A different member of the family gets to plan the activity of the evening each week. The only requirement is that it be a shared activity. I grew up in a family for which the Sunday noon meal was a special family time. Mother most often put a roast in the oven before we left for church. But we all gathered for a delicious meal of roast beef, roasted potatoes with beef gravy, vegetables, salad, hot rolls, homemade pie, the whole thing, around 1:00 P.M. before we even thought about going our separate ways.

For Jan, me, and the kids, the evening mealtime was special. I was always sure to be home from work by 5:00 P.M. even if I had to return later. The kids also knew that, regardless of friends or activities, they were to be home for dinner at 5:00 P.M. It was a time of family prayer. It was also a great time to catch up on what was going on in each other's lives. But unless family time is a priority, it will never happen.

CARVE OUT QUANTITY TIME

We've already addressed the whole quality time versus quantity time issue. The fact is that our kids need both. Perhaps you've read Charley Reece's syndicated column. In a 1996 column he wrote about the best gift for children from their parents. And no, it wasn't a nice house, designer clothes, or a hefty educational account in the bank. Here's what he wrote:

> A friend of mine once taught American history at an expensive private school to sixth graders. One day during a discussion of the Great Depression, she was startled when one of the children said he hoped the United States would have another depression. Several piped up in agreement. When she probed the children with questions, she found out why. At the time, *The Walton's*, a series about a depression-era family, was on network television. 'If we had a depression,' the kids said, 'then perhaps our parents would spend more time with us like they do on *The Walton's*."[3]

Charley Reece went on to comment, "Time is God's currency. One way to think of it is, that when we are born, God opens an account for us and credits us with a finite amount of time. We rarely know the 'account balance.' How we spend this time determines our life."

Again, let me reiterate that quality time is not possible without the investment of quantity time. Simply being physically present is not enough. But without being physically present there will not be the personal interaction, the give and take, the teaching moments, all of which make up quality time. Tragically, many parents rationalize putting in extra hours at the office or on the golf course, or in non-family social activities with the intention of giving undivided attention when they are home, or with a fabulous vacation trip. But it doesn't work that way. For quality time takes place only when both parties are ready for it, not just one. Thus it can't be scheduled.

One of the best ways to provide quality time for your kids is to take them with you when you run errands or even when you go on a business trip. When my kids were growing up I wouldn't even run to the grocery store to pick up some needed item without asking Shan or Jennifer to ride along. And when it didn't greatly interfere with their school and sleep schedule, if I was going on a ministry trip, I would ask one of them to accompany me. Early on my kids were with me on evangelistic calls, pastoral calls, and even hospital calls when appropriate. The conversations that came out of those experiences could not have been manufactured in a sterile "quality time" environment. They came from looking for opportunities just to spend time together.

JUST BE THERE

Just be available! That summarizes most of what I'm trying to say. Early in my ministry I was a workaholic. I still am to a certain extent, but I've placed significant restrictions on it. When Shan was graduating from kindergarten, it was a Tuesday night. That was the same night we had evangelistic calling at the church. This was when our church was still in its infancy and I was the only staff person. I at least had enough fatherly instinct to realize that I should make my evangelistic calls on another night in order to be there for my son's one and only graduation from kindergarten. However, I also felt the obligation to show up and organize and encourage the other callers. I always think I can get more done than is actually humanly possible. I also think it will take me less time to do it. All that resulted in my showing up for Shan's graduation late, as the processional was already in progress. I remember standing at the back of the old Brownsburg Christian Church auditorium and watching my son, Styrofoam mortarboard atop his head, as his eyes searched the audience for his dad; Mom, as always, was already there. When that smile of recognition broke out across his face it did something to my heart that would have a forever impact. For I determined that night that I would never again run the risk of missing out on the significant moments in my children's lives if I could possibly prevent it.

Jan and I have been to hundreds of ballgames, recitals, concerts, open houses, parent-teacher conferences, plays, musicals, contests, and all the rest of the activities that are part and parcel of a modern day, American child's life. On the rare occasions I had to be out of town during such events, my kids understood. But they understood because they knew that I was always otherwise there.

One of my favorite memories of parenting concerns a time I really blew it with my daughter. She was soon to be six years old, a magical birthday. One day, to my horror, I discovered that I had long been scheduled to preach an evangelistic crusade in another state the very week of my daughter's sixth birthday. To this day I have no idea how I made such a scheduling blunder; but it was far too late to reschedule the crusade. So I went to Jennifer and told her, "Daddy's made a terrible mistake. I'm going to have to be out of town on your birthday. But I want to make it up to you. Your birthday is on Monday and I want to take you out on Saturday night, just the two of us, and we'll celebrate your birthday. We'll go any place you want to go and do anything you want to do." It's amazing the promises guilt elicits.

Jennifer's response was, "You mean we can go anywhere?"

"Anywhere!"

"Can we go someplace where you wear a suit and tie and I can wear a dress?"

"Any place you want to go."

"I think I want to go to that place that goes around on top of that hotel downtown." She was referring, of course, to The Eagles Nest high atop the Hyatt. Even back then she had expensive tastes.

But I told her, "Then that's where we'll go."

It was a great evening. I even washed the car. She dressed in a beautiful, frilly, blue dress with polka dots. I dressed up. We used the valet parking and walked into the Hyatt arm in arm. We took the glass-enclosed express elevator to the Eagles Nest where we were escorted to our elegantly set table next to the window giving us a bird's eye view of downtown Indianapolis as dusk was settling in over the city and the lights were beginning to appear. The service staff was especially attentive to my beautiful young date. However, it was only when I was given the menu that I suddenly realized that not only is there no "kiddie menu" in a place like that, there's little or nothing on the menu to appeal to a child.

We settled on prime rib, which I explained to Jennifer as really good roast beef. There would be salad, a baked potato, and some vegetable with a special sauce. Dinner was served. She ate a few bites of "very expensive roast beef," picked at her salad, and had a couple of bites of potato. But somewhere in the hour-long revolution of the restaurant with its spectacular view of the entire city, Jennifer said, "Daddy, I kind of wish we had eaten downstairs."

"Where do you mean, Honey?"

"McDonalds!" At that moment, just prior to the arrival of the check I was wishing the same thing. But after the picked-over meal and dirty dishes were removed, the waiters brought her a piece of cheesecake and somewhere had found a candle they had stuck in it and lighted and, for perhaps the first and last time, the entire service staff of the Eagles Nest sang "Happy Birthday" to a little girl who was turning six.

Our kids and their families now live near us, but even when they lived some distance away, if not on their birthdays, then near their birthdays, we got together and celebrated. If our kids need us, we'll still be there for them. But being there is especially important in those growing up years. And dads, it's not just important for Mom to be there, but for you to be there too. Researchers have found that there is a high correlation between homes disrupted by a father's absence and just about every social problem you can imagine.

So be there for those programs, games, and concerts. It won't always be easy. At one time school administrators had respect for Sunday and Wednesday night programming in churches. That has all but eroded away in recent years. My daughter's last two years in high school band concerts were scheduled on Wednesday nights. Not only that, but her senior year Jennifer had the piccolo solo on "Stars and Stripes Forever." In each case I went to the concert, took in as much of the music as possible, including my daughter's solo, and then drove to the church where the music minister was "vamping" until I could arrive to preach.

I mentioned in an earlier chapter Jan's practice of debriefing with the kids each day after school. Kathi Hunter said that this time was for her and her kids the "after-school coffee break." After the kids had put away their backpacks and petted the dog, they would gather around the kitchen table where she prepared popcorn, hot chocolate, cookies or pretzels, and lemonade. There she would learn about the day's happenings, how much homework had to be done, and most importantly, how she could pray for her kids.[4]

Bedtime is also an important time just to be there. It's a time to review the events of the day, pray together, and enjoy one of the most unguarded times of the day for a child. It's an awesome time for answering questions for young children or listening to experiences of the day that if not reviewed will simply get lost in the busyness of life. From sitting on the bed reading bedtime stories to a small child to sprawling on the floor or leaning up against the wall of a teenager's room and just listening, bedtime can make a powerful difference in both your child's life and your own. And don't forget the hugs and kisses, even when they object.

There may be no time when it is more important for you to simply be there than those times in which your children are hurting. Those hurts take many different forms all the way from being called a bad name by a so-called friend during recess to getting cut from the team to not getting invited to join the "in group" to being turned down for a date to the death of a friend. I still grieve when I remember the day Shan's friends came to our house to tell him that one of his closest friends had taken his own life the night before. I've never seen my son in such pain. There was really nothing we could say, but we could be there.

When children, younger or older, hurt, they need someone to hold them, to listen to them, to offer advice when requested, but mostly just to be there. And I'm not just talking about physical presence, but also being open and sensitive to them, understanding of them, and most of all, not minimizing their pain or the significance of their hurt. When your child is hurting, stop whatever you are doing and empathize with what he or she is going through and reaffirm your love and concern. Again, let me point out that this is no time to find fault with the child, i.e., "If you'd listened to me this never would have happened." This is no time to belittle the crisis, i.e., "Hey, it's really no big deal, you'll get over it." This is a time to just be there with understanding, sympathy, and love.

I realize that in making this point some of you may be feeling that I'm trying to put a guilt trip on you because the realities of life are that you have to travel a great deal or work long hours or otherwise not be available to your kids through no fault of your own. But all of us have a certain amount of discretionary time, even if it's limited. So work on maximizing the use of that time in being there for your kids. You may have to play less golf, cut down on social engagements, turn off the TV, or even turn down a service opportunity at church. And when it comes to comparing the economic benefit to your children by your taking that promotion as opposed to the time benefit to your children by turning it down, you will rarely, if ever, regret the latter.

Dr. Laura had a listener who struggled with self-pity over the sacrifices he made for his children until he really came to grips with what it meant to be a dad. He put his thoughts into poetic form:

When I became a father,
I gave up everything . . .
I gave up sleeping in on weekends . . .
now, we make our weekly early morning "pig adventure" walk to get
     bagels, make cream cheese lips and find out how many ways we can
     spill chocolate milk.
I gave up my beautiful sports car . . .
now, we pile into the van for a messy, cookie crumbled, sticky-fingered,
wet-bottomed, sandy-footed, laugh filled trip to and from the beach.
I gave up workouts at the club, now, I hold my little girl on my lap on my
     home workout machine, as we sing, "Row, Row, Row Your Boat."
I have given up sleeping through the night . . .
now, I get to wake up after an unsettling dream of attacking lobsters,
     chasing snakes or talking teddy bears wakes up my son, and I rock
     him to sleep in my arms and feel his gentle breath on my neck.
I gave up quiet, candle-lit dinners with my wife . . .
now, I serve the umpteenth version of "Chicken Nuggets du Jour" and
     try not to show a smile as milk squirts from the noses of the laughing
     faces gathered around me at the table.
I gave up watching the nightly news . . .

now, I smile in amazed wonder as my kids and I laugh together at the
same "George of the Jungle" cartoons I watched 25 years ago.
I gave up having extra, expendable income . . .
now, I have treasures I cannot even begin to count.
When I gave up everything...I became a Dad...[5]

HAVE A DATE NIGHT

Let me devote at least a couple of paragraphs to a special kind of "being there" for dads in particular, and that's what I call date nights. When my kids were growing up, I devoted one night a week to doing something special with my kids individually. Obviously this works better with two kids than ten. Although Shan and I would never have called it date night, that's what it was, because it was a dedicated date on my calendar. With him it wasn't necessarily a certain night of the week. But we planned ahead for ballgames, movies, a hike in the park, or just dinner together, preferably at Acapulco Joe's with the finest Mexican food in the East. I remember the hours we spent in line to see the first showing of the latest "Star Wars" movie and scalping tickets for the Cardinals/Cubs game at Wrigley Field that went 17 innings. There were concerts like Petra in Terre Haute or U-2 at the Dome. Yes, I would have flicked my Bic if I had one. But the bonding that went on during those special times is worth far more than any monetary price.

With Jennifer, our date night has always been Thursday. It began while she was still a preschooler. Again, it was sometimes as involved as a trip to another city for a special attraction or as simple as going to Dairy Queen for a Blizzard, that was pre-Glacier days at Ritters. Movies—we often saw the sad ones and both of us would cry and hold each other—concerts of all sorts, circuses, ice shows, and all sorts of attractions filled our date nights. Sometimes it was IU Basketball or a Pacers' game. But more often than not it was dinner at a nice restaurant. We looked for unique, out-of-the way places, or perhaps the atmosphere of a Broad Ripple sidewalk café. Again, it wasn't the location or activity as much as it was simply being together.

When she reached her teen years, Jennifer never lacked for male attention. But I can remember on several occasions hearing her turn down a date by saying, "Thursday night? No, that's my night to spend with my Daddy." Again, as a current commercial says, "Priceless!" Now that Jennifer is married and has a career, date nights are out. However, we have our revised version. At least once a year we go away, just the two of us, most often to an amusement park, and just hang out together for a couple of days. Recently, rather than an amusement park it was a trip to Chicago for sightseeing, seeing "The Lion King" theatrical production at the Cadillac Palace Theater, fun at Navy Pier, and shopping on "The Magnificent Mile."

I share all that not to brag on my parenting skills, for there are so many ways in which I could have and should have been a better father, but I share it because it is without a doubt one of the best things I ever did as a father, and I highly recommend it to others.

MAKE FAMILY ACTIVITIY A HIGH PRIORITY

We live in an overextended, overcommitted, overworked, overstressed society. In order to make family activity a priority we must discipline ourselves to say no to many opportunities that come our way. Quite frankly, that is difficult, especially for committed Christians. There are so many needs crying out for attention as well as so many opportunities to do things we would really enjoy doing. But the first three priorities in each of our lives ought to be God first, spouse second, and children third. So prioritizing family time is an absolute necessity. Make commitments to your family and then stick with those commitments no matter how hard they may be to keep.

How will your children remember you? What sort of memory album are you compiling as a family? The things we're talking about are not simply matters of getting your kids raised, but of what sort of lives they are going to lead. Memories are powerful forces in shaping lives. Robert Bruce, in his book, *Reclaiming Your Family*, writes, "Our memories are a lot like sinkholes or volcanoes. On the surface there is the obvious hole in the ground; you can see it and measure it. But these surface features are only the beginning; in fact, the surface is merely the by product of what is going on deep down inside."[6] Good memories form the basis for a good life.

So an important part of parenting is shaping memories. I hope your kids will have loads of good ones centered on all sorts of quality and quantity time experiences with mom and dad. Yes, Jan and I have made lots of mistakes. But I know our children have absolutely no doubt as to our unconditional love for them. And because of how we prioritized even the time we spent with them, they also know we love God with all our hearts and are committed disciples of Jesus Christ. If they thought we were fun, too—at least most of the time—then that's the icing on the cake.

Chapter Four

Have Fun

Some of the principles I'm sharing, if practiced, reap wonderful dividends; however, the practice of those principles is hard work and a heavy responsibility. In this chapter I will spotlight a responsibility that is an immediate win/win. The kids enjoy it immediately as do the parents. I'm talking about the principle of having fun.

One of the negative results of becoming empty nesters is that you have a lot of excuses taken away for simply being silly and doing fun things that no serious, sober adult would ever do on their own. I mean, a parent can buy toys for their kids that the parent always wanted, play with the toys, and appear that they're just being good parents rather than selfish, foolish adults. A parent can go to amusement parks and circuses and have a ball—all in the name of loving their kids. But when the kids grow up and leave home, the excuses are gone. That's just one of the reasons I thank God for grandkids!

The truth is, having fun comes very naturally for some but is a real effort for others. Yet fun is an important part of raising "G-Rated" kids. I know you will find this hard to believe, but I'm not always the life of the party. Sometimes I take myself too seriously. I have a built-in excuse as the pastor of a large church to carry the weight of the world on my shoulders. And to my shame, I admit that there were plenty of times while my kids were growing up that I was quiet, withdrawn, and grumpy. Jan used to joke that "Daddy keeps his sense of humor in a suitcase," and she would tease me, "Come on, open your suitcase." When I really abandoned my pastoral façade and allowed myself simply to really have fun, the kids often said, "Wow, Dad's really got his suitcase open tonight!"

Some children never hear their parents laugh or really have fun. While it might seem presumptuous—even ludicrous—for someone like me to try to tell you how to have fun, the fact is that we did have fun, and I believe we provided an environment for many other positive things to take place. So chill out, parents, and have some fun. Learn to laugh at yourself. As someone once said, "Don't be too cool to be a fool!" Our kids need to see us let our hair down, be vulnerable, take chances, get real, relax, and have fun. A side benefit will be that your kids learn that growing up doesn't necessarily mean always being serious and uptight.

LEARN TO HAVE FUN

Parents who can laugh and play with their kids become real rather than merely authority figures and disciplinarians. When children are very young this can mean tickle wrestling, peek-a-boo, and toys. It progresses to hide-and-seek, tag, ring-around-the-rosie and other such games. Shan and my daughter-in-law Lise had their version of hide-and-seek they played with our first grandson when he was only one year old. He would go into another room and they would take a favorite toy and hide it, usually in plain sight. Then they would count to ten and say, "Ready or not here Jack comes!" He would run giggling into the room, stand in the middle of the floor, and look all around until he spotted the toy, then run and grab it while everyone applauded and yelled, "Yea, Jack!" Yes, he had a wonderful time, but so did his parents and occasionally his grandparents as well.

As children grow older there are board games, card games, playing catch, riding a bike, shooting baskets, special trips, and the list goes on and on. Having fun with our children means relaxing and not taking their growing pains or our own lives too seriously. It means leaving our work at work, abandoning concerns about dignity, and getting on their level. It means laughing together and remembering that whatever the activity, the object is to have fun together, not to win.

Although I've never been athletic, I've always been competitive. In my son's early athletic adventures my competitiveness translated into less-than-best behavior on my part on the sidelines or in the stands. When he and I competed one-on-one in any sport early on, I could dominate simply by virtue of size. But it didn't take long for him to catch up and pass me in most athletic endeavors. Thankfully, by that time I had learned for myself and taught him as well that we should play hard, play fair, have fun, and win or lose graciously.

Good parents want their kids to be emotionally strong, well adjusted, and have healthy attitudes toward their parents. I believe that learning to chill out, have fun, abandon pretense, and simply be real are important elements of making that happen.

PLAY WITH YOUR CHILDREN

We live in a fallen world. Satan's desire is to steal everything good and wholesome. Let's face it, most of "World News Tonight" is not joyful or playful. I don't believe it is over-spiritualizing to say that playing with your kids is in itself an act of faith and defiance of evil.

I've already stressed the importance of playing games or tossing a ball around. Play brings to mind dolls and sandboxes, trips to the park, and reading entertaining stories. But even work can become play when weeding the flowerbed becomes a game or results in a laugh-filled "weed-fight" concluded with play wrestling on the lawn. Keep in mind that the process, the playing itself, is far more important than the outcome. Sure you could weed a flowerbed far more efficiently on your own than you could by involving your child in the process; but what you would miss out on is far more significant.

Play, by its very definition, is not intended to be efficient. You can take a walk on your own and go faster and further and perhaps even receive more physical benefit than if you have a small child tagging along. Jan and I recently took our grandson, Jack, on a nature trail. It wasn't a physically demanding or efficient hike. But we saw wooly worms, we threw walnuts, we picked up leaves, we looked under rocks, and we saw a whole different world that we had forgotten existed. Again, the process is far more important than the outcome, the efficiency, or the apparent result.

Playing with your children or grandchildren is an investment of time and energy that pays high dividends—although not quickly observable ones. But the bonding, the affirmation, the valuing, as well as the pure delight and enjoyment are all dividends that are reinvested and come back with compound interest.

"Look at me, Mommy!" "Daddy, watch!" Play is meant to capture your attention. When we take our two-year-old grandson to the park, and I put Will in the swing, on every push he says, "Higher, please! Higher, please, Paw-Paw!" That's not so much a tribute to his daring as a request for my continued attention. And that's no different than his daddy before him at the same age yelling, "Daddy, watch!" as he prepared to jump off a step from the stupendous height of eighteen inches. It's the same with my little girl dressed as a ballerina or playing in her first piano recital, or my son in his T-ball uniform. "Watch, Mom and Dad, I'm about to do something very special. Do you see me? Am I important? Do you value me?"

Dr. Dan Allender, wrote in *How Children Raise Parents*, "Amazement is the antechamber of admiration. To admire is to humble oneself before the splendor and glory of another... Admiration blesses the other as being and becoming what we are not. It names uniqueness without attempting to bring it down to our status. It is the finest form of accolade."[1]

Playing with your children is one of the greatest affirmations of admiration. Your children long to be the pride of your life, not because of their performance, but just because of their being.

Most parents "play" with their children when they are little. Tragically, many parents abandon such play as their children grow older. But a child's need for attention, admiration, and affirmation doesn't end at five—or even fifty. I know of many 50-year-old adults who are still striving to receive their parents' admiration—admiration they never received as children. That is sad indeed—not that they are seeking it, but that it was never given. Playing with your children gives you a beautiful, pressure-free environment for giving attention, expressing admiration, and giving affirmation.

LOOK FOR EXCUSES TO CELEBRATE

Play is important, but it is only one of many ways to have fun. If you want to have fun it is often helpful to have a good excuse for that fun. In short, find a reason to celebrate. God loves celebration; that's one reason He gave the Jewish nation so many feast days and festivals to keep. And I believe a family should seize on every opportunity it gets to celebrate.

Did your child get an A on the big test? Surely that deserves a celebration. How about the fact that they've solved a difficult problem or completed a project? Milestones like completing another grade level in school, moving up a class in swimming lessons, or receiving another merit badge give you an excuse to have a celebration. We always looked for any reason to have a celebration around our house; and it is important to celebrate not just performance but character. A child making his or her bed and keeping his or her room straight may have been a far greater achievement for that child than making an A on a test or winning the big ballgame.

If celebrations are reserved only for winning, some kids will never get to experience a celebration. When Kingsway Christian School began its sport participation, we were beaten in every area of competition. Shan played on a school soccer team from the beginning. It wasn't much fun getting slaughtered game after game, but we celebrated good sportsmanship, good effort, and the completion of a season. "Ice cream for everyone" didn't require a win.

Make sure you make a big deal out of the holidays and special days as well. Birthdays—both physical and spiritual, Christmas, Easter, Independence Day, Mother's Day, Father's Day, Memorial Day, Thanksgiving, Valentine's Day, graduations, you name it and it's an opportunity for a celebration. According to Fred Hartley in *Parenting At Its Best*, researchers have found in studying dysfunctional families that one of the most obvious characteristics is the inability to celebrate. Instead,

"For dysfunctional families, weddings, birthdays, and other celebrative moments degenerate into interpersonal disasters."[2]

FIND HOBBIES TO SHARE

Hobbies provide an enjoyable, non-threatening way for parents to interact with their children. From collecting coins, stamps, baseball cards, or model planes to doing crafts, reading, playing instruments, listening to music, or going to movies, there are many wonderful ways to have fun with your kids while pursuing a hobby.

Some of the best of times for our family involved the children's involvement in music. Shan played the trumpet and Jennifer played the piano and flute. Recitals and music contests gave way to marching band competitions. But we were always there, sharing as a family. Even in times of disappointment there was the comfort and encouragement of family, even as there was great celebration in successes. And in it all there was fun.

DEVELOP FAMILY TRADITIONS

Traditions are simply family celebrations and/or practices that are repeated again and again. But traditions are also like special cords that bind a family together. It's up to you to choose what those traditions will be; but holidays just beg for a family to begin traditions.

Christmas is my favorite time of the year; and it has always been a tradition-filled time for our family. We started taking our kids to Watt's Christmas Tree Farm early on where we picked out and cut our own tree. The trip home with the tree necessitated a stop at Mr. Dan's, for Coney dogs. Unfortunately that part of the tradition stopped when Mr. Dan's went out of business. We all had our specific jobs to do in putting up and decorating the tree. Homemade Christmas cookies have long been a part of our celebration. We played the same Christmas music year after year and watched the same Christmas movies together. There was and still is the yearly trip to see all the beautifully decorated neighborhoods. When the kids were younger we always took them to Santa Land at Ayres for a ride on the Santa Express and a session with the jolly old elf himself.

Now we are sure to take Jack and Will to the Indiana State Museum reproduction of Ayres Santa Land.

Christmas at the Zoo has long been a part of our early Christmas tradition. It should be noted that traditions should serve us rather than the reverse. One year the temperature was hovering at zero but I was determined to preserve the tradition. Jan and Jennifer backed out; but Shan and I, the men of the family, pressed on. Actually Christmas at the Zoo was closed but after sufficient begging from yours truly they let us take a quick walk around. We nearly froze to death. It was not a good decision, but we preserved the tradition.

Of course there are all sorts of Christmas Day traditions at our house. There's the special cranberry tea Jan fixes, the aroma of which fills the house early that morning. There's the picture taken of the kids beneath the Christmas tree, which has become kids, spouses, and grandkids. There's the reading of the Christmas story, thankfully still printed in the *Indianapolis Star*, though no longer on the front page. There are the Christmas stockings, the calendars, the nuts, the comic books, and, of course, the gift exchange with everyone waiting until the person before them has opened and oohed and aahed over the gift before opening another.

From coloring Easter eggs to returning to the same vacation spot year after year; from the Thanksgiving afternoon viewing of the latest holiday kids movie to homemade banana ice cream on Memorial Day; from 4th of July concerts and fireworks downtown or at Conner Prairie, to everyone being home at 5:00 P.M. for dinner around the table, our kids were brought up governed by and enjoying—for the most part—any number of family traditions.

TAKE THOSE VACATIONS

Without a doubt, if you were to ask our kids for their favorite "growing up" memories, they would tell you about our family vacations. Neither Jan nor I grew up in families that took vacations. The closest thing to a vacation at our house was the once-a-year pilgrimage to Minnesota to visit my Uncle Paul and his family. That was fun because Uncle Paul was fun. He was a pilot with his own plane. He had a cabin on a lake. He was a Ham radio operator. We were always going places when we were at his place. And best of all, my Aunt Ruth made the best chocolate pie in the world. But aside from a few days at Thanksgiving or Christmas, the home in which I grew up was vacation free.

There was one exception. The summer after I graduated from high school Dad took off three weeks from his business, unprecedented, and took my mother and me on a trip out west where we took in the sights of Rocky Mountain National Park, my first taste of Wyoming with the Grand Tetons and Yellowstone, the desert beauty of Nevada and Utah, and even the Grand Canyon. I treasure that trip in part because it was so unique. I can still see my dad driving up Trail Ridge Road, stopping on the Continental Divide for the first time, and I remember my first glimpse of the incredible Old Faithful Lodge. But I wish there would have been more such times.

Soon after Jan and I were first married we began traveling in full-time evangelistic work. For us, a vacation had nothing to do with travel, it was getting to stay home. But even as we traveled across the country for six years, we took advantage of the opportunity to see the sights and experience many things most people never get to experience. And since I held crusades from coast to coast and border to border, we got to scout out the country and see the places we wanted to come to again.

Of all the places we went and all the things we saw, the Grand Tetons in Wyoming were and are our favorite. So when we came off the road and into located ministry, it was to the Tetons that we found ourselves returning again and again. Actually, we went there every other year during the years that our kids were growing up. We always went to the same lodge, Signal Mountain. And we did many of the same things again and again: scenic float trips on the Snake River, hiking in the mountains, early morning trail rides to a hot breakfast prepared over an open fire, shopping in Jackson, white water rafting for the more adventurous, that means everyone but Jan, and mealtimes at Bubba's and Billy's.

Of course, there was always a trip to the Bar-J Ranch for barbecue and western music. On weekends there was worship at the Jackson Community Church, and sometimes campground vespers as well. Since the Community Church didn't celebrate the Lord's Supper each weekend, there was also the Caldwell family communion service in which we all had a part.

There are lots of wonderful memories in all that. But the greatest blessings came from simply having time together, meaningful times for deep discussions of important issues, and silly times for laughing ourselves sick. We have stories to tell that not only will I be repeating till they put me in the grave, but my kids will tell to their kids who in turn will tell them to theirs. There's my foolish 13-mile hike down a mountain in cowboy boots that resulted in blisters, foolish pride, passed over opportunities, and eventual rescue by my kids. There's the Dad and Shan Paintbrush Divide adventure; and Jennifer's rediscovery of Lard Bucket (sorry, too complicated to tell). There are bear, moose, and buffalo stories as well as runaway horse stories. But all this is part of the fabric of who we are as a family. Our kids continued to work their schedules so they could vacation with us through their college years with rare exceptions.

It always amazed me how the children of some of our contemporaries would do anything to get out of a family vacation. I wonder if it wasn't in part because Mom and Dad planned vacations around things they wanted to do rather than what the kids would enjoy. Jan and I had a ball, but family vacations were more focused on what the kids wanted to do. Jan and I have the rest of our lives to do what we want to do on vacation, and we're doing that now. But make sure family vacations are fun for everyone.

By the way, the year we didn't go to the Tetons, we went somewhere completely different. Because I've been actively involved in the North American Christian Convention over the years, and it is a summertime convention, we would most often allow the location of the convention to at least influence where we would vacation before or after the convention. And there were and are always mini-vacations like an overnight trip to a state park. We've hiked every trail at McCormick's Creek, Brown County, and Turkey Run State Parks. Amusement parks have always been big with the three more adventuresome members of our clan—although Jan was always a good sport, and someone had to watch our stuff while we were on the newest, biggest, fastest, highest roller coaster. There were also special trips. I took Shan with me to Israel when he was 12 and Jennifer when she was 16. Those trips weren't just fun, they were inspirational and life-changing.

EMPHASIZE FAMILY

In our increasingly fragmented society it is more and more imperative that we teach our children the value and importance of family; and not just our immediate family but our extended family of grandparents, aunts, uncles, and cousins as well. Family heritage is something to be taught and celebrated. Jan's genealogical research into both sides of our family has helped us appreciate who we are. Family reunions, planned and formal or unplanned and spontaneous, are a great environment to not only have fun but to celebrate family as well.

But for your immediate family, family mealtimes, setting aside a family night, playing together from Putt-Putt to table games or video games are all important in strengthening those bonds that are so important. I know that busyness works against us. But it's all a matter of priorities. So take time for family fun and traditions. How about adopting a needy family during the holiday season or adopting a patient at a local nursing home. Some of our families at church spend every Thanksgiving feeding the homeless at inner city missions.

Whatever you do, don't let the years get away. Your one-year-old will never learn to walk again. Your two- or three-year-old will never be a toddler again. There'll never be another first day of school. There won't be another second grade play or middle school band concert. So be there.

MAKE MEMORIES

There are many things Jan and I could have done better as parents. But I'm so thankful for the things we did right. As a result, we have enough memories that we could feed off of them until Jesus comes. But the truth of the matter is that we are still making new ones all the time.

I think of the silly pet names we adopted for each other, of taking our hound dog, Charlie, down the curly slide at McCormick's Creek, of wading in mud through the canyon at Turkey Run, of building a wooden play set with and for my five-year-old son in our backyard (the only thing I ever built). I remember snowball fights, snow tunnels, and snow ice cream, shooting hoops or playing catch, hidden Easter eggs and homemade valentines. There was a candlelight dinner with my six-year-old daughter atop the Hyatt in the Eagles Nest, birthday parties at Farrell's Ice Cream Parlor. I thank God for each and every memory.

Don't miss out. Take time to have fun. Celebrate family and make memories.

Chapter Five

Provide Discipline

I can see him as though it was yesterday. Our five-year-old son was standing on the very edge of our yard, feet planted firmly on the boundary, looking longingly into our neighbor's yard where the neighborhood children had gathered to play. We had just moved to 3 Sheffield Court in Avon, Indiana, to begin our ministry with the infant Kingsway Christian Church. One of the strongly enforced ground rules was that Shan was not to leave our yard for any reason without specific permission.

So there he was, pushing the rule to the limit, going as far as he could within the rules, but still obeying his mom and dad. Did he understand the reason for the rule? Probably not. Did he want to break the rule? Absolutely! Was he obeying out of love and respect for his parents? If those things entered into his obedience at all, it was a very subliminal thing. No, he knew that the authority figures in his life had forbidden him to cross that boundary, and he knew there would be very unpleasant consequences if he disobeyed.

Were we being unfair to him, just throwing our weight around, and arousing unnecessary fears in the heart of an innocent five-year-old child? The truth is, we loved our son and wanted to protect him from numerous dangers he was far too young to understand. Rather than being unfair to him, we were obligated by love to provide and enforce boundaries that would both protect and guide him into the future. Later that day I hugged him and told him how proud I was of him for obeying even though I knew it was very difficult; and I reaffirmed what he could still not fully comprehend, that the rules were for his good and his protection.

The story is told of how the mother of George Washington was seated next to a distinguished French general at a state banquet when the general turned and asked her, "How did you ever manage to raise such a noble son?" Without hesitation she replied, "I taught him to obey." She understood the principle of providing discipline that is so sadly missing in many homes today, even Christian homes.

Let's set the record straight right from the beginning, God's Word teaches the obligation of parents to provide loving discipline:

> My child, don't ignore it when the LORD disciplines you, and don't be discouraged when He corrects you. For the Lord corrects those He loves, just as a father corrects a child in whom he delights (Prov. 3:11-12).

> If you refuse to discipline your children, it proves you don't love them; if you love your children you will be prompt to discipline them" (Prov. 13:24). The Lord disciplines those He loves, and He punishes those He accepts as His children. As you endure this divine discipline, remember that God is treating you as His own children. Whoever heard of a child who was never disciplined? If God doesn't discipline you as He does all of His children, it means that you are illegitimate and are not really His children at all. Since we respect our earthly fathers who disciplined us, should we not all the more cheerfully submit to the discipline of our heavenly Father and live forever?
>
> (Heb. 12:6-9)

> Discipline your children while there is hope. If you don't you will ruin their lives.
>
> (Prov. 19:18)

And now a word to you fathers. Don't make your children angry by the way you treat them. Rather, bring them up with the discipline and instruction approved by the Lord.

(Eph. 6:4)

Over the years I've counseled with many parents who are heartbroken because of a wayward child. I've never had any say, "Pastor, I just wish I hadn't been so strong in my discipline." I've never had any parent of a prodigal son or daughter say, "All those scriptures on discipline, they're just not true."

A pastor called together the parents in his congregation whose children had recently reached adulthood. He asked those parents what they would do differently if they had it all to do over again. Listen to these responses:

"I'd be tougher. I was afraid of my child when he was younger, and now he doesn't respect me, as he should. I would be firm and in control."

"I would not give in as much. I feel as if there is always pressure to do what the other parents allow for their teen. I would stick with the rules that were appropriate for our family."

"I would not be so concerned about what others think when I grounded my daughter or made her do family activities instead of going off with peers. I would think first of our family and what is right for us."

"I would not feel so guilty all the time for disciplining my sons. I realize that this is my duty to be in control of my family, and I wouldn't care what others thought as I raised my children in a disciplined manner."[1]

It is my hope that you can be spared the disappointments of others by learning from their mistakes.

BOUNDARIES ARE IMPORTANT

Can you imagine a life without boundaries? It would be chaotic, dangerous, and destructive. Speed limits are boundaries to keep us from killing each other on the highways. Walls are boundaries to protect that which is within and keep out that which is without. Balcony railings are boundaries to keep us from falling and hurting ourselves, and so are fences along cliffs in popular parks. A number of years ago, the teenaged son of one of our faithful families free-fell 50 feet off a cliff at Turkey Run State Park. He survived, but he broke nearly every bone in his body. He could have used a protective boundary that day.

Even the games we play require boundaries. Can you imagine a football, soccer, or basketball game in which the participants were free to go anywhere and throw or kick the ball anywhere? Again, there wouldn't even be a game under such circumstances. There would only be chaos and confusion. Boundaries are important in every aspect of life. A river without boundaries is a destructive flood. And families without boundaries are confused, insecure, and headed for trouble.

By the way, boundaries come in both negative and positive varieties. There are the negative boundaries that tell us what we can't do and where we can't go, which are rules and regulations. But there are also the positive guidelines that tell us what we can and should do, which are our guidelines and goals.

What are some of the areas in which boundaries should be established for your family? We are going to look at three areas later.

There are *absolutes*. These are moral issues such as lying, stealing, dishonoring parents, and purposeful disobedience.

Then there are *ground rules*. These are made up of mealtimes, homework, household chores, curfews, and other things on which you as a family have to determine your own boundaries.

There are also areas of *grace* where the preference is made clear but children are allowed some latitude.

Such boundaries should not simply be arbitrary but should serve a purpose, the first of which is to protect physically, spiritually, emotionally, and morally. They also provide a feeling of security in which children are free to flourish because they know where they stand. If a child is old enough to understand, the boundaries need to be explained, not only as to the purpose of the boundary but also as to the consequences of violating the boundaries. Of course, the consequences should fit the violation. I remember when the preschool son of our youth pastor used a vulgar slang expression in front of God, his parents, and even the senior pastor and his wife. After the initial shock, Andy took him aside and asked him where he had heard that expression. It turns out he had just returned from accompanying his father on a junior high trip. Enough said? So the father explained why we don't say that and told him if he said it again he would be punished. Innocence wasn't punished, but willful disobedience would be.

It is also important for parents to recognize the difference between a careless act and a defiant act. I've seen toddlers accidentally knock over a glass of milk; certainly not a punishable offense. But I've also seen toddlers reach out and intentionally knock over a glass of milk. It often happens in the presence of guests and the child is testing the boundaries, seeing what he or she can get by with. That is a punishable offense. Actually, the defiant attitude is a far greater problem than the act itself.

Whatever the appropriate punishment, the parent should remain calm, cool, and serious. Point out the act of disobedience, carry out the punishment, repeat the reason for the punishment, and then reaffirm the parent's love for the child. Don't argue, don't scream or yell, just do what is right. What is the appropriate punishment? That will vary according to the severity of the offense and the age of the child. It could range from a verbal rebuke to hand-slapping to spanking to time out to taking away privileges to grounding to something much more creative.

It should also be pointed out that the boundaries change with the maturing of the child. The "don't leave the yard without permission" boundary for our preschoolers was phased out long before adolescence. However, the "no R-rated movie" boundary was in place by the time they reached adolescence. Most people would consider us pretty strict parents, but if you were to ask our children today you would find out they were thankful for our strictness. Oh, they tested it. They pushed the boundaries. That's a normal part of growing up. But they also knew that those boundaries gave them protection and security. As a matter of fact, on several occasions each of our children came to us and said, "So and so wants us to do such and such. We can't do that can we, Dad?" That was always their way of requesting that their parents get them off the hook. They were looking for a crutch to take the pressure off of them to do something they knew was questionable. Parents should be glad to provide such a crutch.

The idea is that there are strict boundaries early on, boundaries the child may not even understand. There are different boundaries later, but boundaries that are understandable and that allow for some input on the part of the child. As adolescence progresses, if the child has proven to be worthy of trust, more and more boundaries are removed and more and more responsibility is given, preparing for the child to be on his or her own. But there are certain boundaries that are absolutes and thus never removed. There are even ground rules that may be and should be maintained by the parents. Sometimes kids leave home and then come back again, chiefly because of economic necessity; but they feel they have the right to come and go as they please and do as they please. Oh, no! In the words of my father, "As long as you live in our house you will live by our rules!"

SHOULD WE SPANK?

There are few subjects that provoke as much emotional response in regard to parenting as does spanking. I've gotten my share of critical letters over the years but none stronger or more emotional than one from a young man, newly married, with no children. I was not even preaching on parenting, but as an aside I had said that people who did not love their children enough to discipline them didn't truly love them. I made some reference to spanking in that context and this young man went ballistic. He rebuked me soundly for preaching my opinion, saying that there was absolutely no biblical basis for what I was teaching. When I responded with a letter citing scripture after scripture, he never got back to me. Instead he and his wife simply left the church.

To this day, I have no idea why this subject was such a hot button one with him. But he is not alone. In researching the material for this book I ran across several Christian authors and parenting experts who not only condemned the practice of spanking but of any form of punishment. One such expert devotes an entire chapter to "Why Punishment Doesn't Work." Of course, these conclusions come not from studying God's Word, but from buying into the politically correct thought on parenting that now stretches back two generations to the teaching of Dr. Benjamin Spock. The idea is that spanking only leads to anger, resentment, and inner rebellion. Child psychology courses took up that cause and parents and educators swallowed that poison. We no longer spanked the child's hands when he did wrong, we took the paddle out of the classroom, and the bite out of the law.

By the way, many child psychologists have changed their tune. A 2002 report to the American Psychological Association meeting in San Francisco concluded that spanking "...does not hurt youngsters' social or emotional development... A lot of people out there advocate that any spanking at all is detrimental, and that's not what we found. We're not advocating this is a strategy that should be used with kids, but we object to people wanting to ban it when we see no evidence that it's harmful."[2]

Many who were of the initial generation brought up on Dr. Spock are the ones who later held college administrators hostage, set fire to shopping centers, and rioted in the streets. And though spanking was supposed to cause those kids to hate their parents, the fact is that they hated them anyway. Rebellion tolerated at an early age only escalates as a child grows older. The preschooler who stomps his foot and throws a tantrum to get his way, if indulged, will next be challenging the teachers, then the police, then society, but ultimately God. And such a child will have no respect whatsoever for his or her parents.

Not only does God's Word allow for the practice of punishment, it actually says, "If you refuse to discipline your children, it proves you don't love them; if you love your children, you will be prompt to discipline them" (Prov. 13:24). The *New American Standard Bible* reads, "He who spares his rod hates his son, But he who loves him disciplines him diligently." I think it is significant that back when Jennifer was still in high school and Shan in college and I asked my children to provide me with a list of things Jan and I did right as parents, high on Shan's list was, "They taught me to respect authority and enforced that respect, i.e. Woody the Spoon." More on Woody later.

Now, I'm certainly not arguing for the indiscriminate use of corporal punishment. Personally, I believe it should be reserved for particularly grievous offenses such as lying and intentional disobedience. But because the practice is under such assault, I'm devoting more space to the subject than would otherwise be the case.

Eight Benefits of Discipline by Spanking

A well-known but now-deceased pastor wrote a book many years ago in which he pointed out eight specific benefits of spanking, all taken directly from God's Word. The points are his. The scriptures are God's. The comments are mine.[3]

1. **The parent who spanks the child teaches him to have wisdom.** "To discipline and reprimand a child produces wisdom, but a mother is disgraced by an undisciplined child (Prov. 29:15).

    Actually, the NLT softens that verse. Here's the more literal rendering from the NASB: "The rod and reproof give wisdom, but a child who gets his own way brings shame to his mother."

    There is great wisdom in understanding that disobedience brings punishment. It's true at school. It's true in society. It's also true in our relationship with God, "For the wages of sin is death" (Rom. 6:23). How much better it is for the child to gain that wisdom at home and thus associate disobedience and wrong with punishment and therefore do his best to avoid it.

2. **The parent who spanks his child provides himself with a happy future.** "But a mother is disgraced by an undisciplined child."

    As a pastor I have counseled many a heartbroken parent who failed to properly discipline his or her child when the opportunity presented itself. Many such parents never hear from their children or even know where they are. Meanwhile, many of the parents who learned the truth of Prov. 29:15 in time enjoy the pride of seeing their children become responsible citizens and loving children.

3. **The parent who spanks his child guarantees him a clean life.** "Physical punishment cleanses away evil; such discipline purifies the heart" (Prov. 20:30).

    As we learned in chapter one, many of these proverbs are truisms, observations of the way things most generally are as a result of the principle taught. So the word "guarantee" may be too strong.

But there is definitely a connection between loving discipline and learning that sin has negative consequences. I was taught at church that certain behaviors are wrong; I had that teaching reinforced at home by the application of the wild cherry switch to the back of my legs. Again, the child learns to fear and hate disobedience because it always brings him trouble and even pain.

4. **The parent who spanks his child offers for himself more opportunities for service to God.** "(An elder) must manage his own family well, with children who respect and obey him. For if a man cannot manage his own household, how can he take care of God's church?" (1 Tim. 3:4-5).

    The man who does not follow God's plan for discipline is disqualified for leadership in the Lord's church. But this is an age old principle well illustrated in the Old Testament as well. For instance, Abraham was blessed and used of God in a great way, in part because Gen. 18:19 says of him, "I [God] have singled him out so that he will direct his sons and their families to keep the way of the Lord and do what is right and just." On the other hand, Eli, the high priest in Samuel's day, forfeited God's blessing upon his life because God said of him, "I have warned him continually that judgment is coming for his family, because his sons are blaspheming God and he hasn't disciplined them" (1 Sam. 3:13).

5. **The disciplining parent adds years to the life of his child.** "Honor your father and mother. Then you will live a long, full life in the land the Lord your God will give you" (Ex. 20:12).

    Here we have another truism. Children who are disciplined by their parents and thus learn to honor and obey their parents are far less likely to be involved in behaviors that might prematurely end their lives. Disciplining your child may very well add years to his or her life. The apostle Paul reiterates this teaching in the New Testament: "Honor your father and mother.' This is the first of the Ten Commandments that ends with a promise. And this is the promise: If you honor your father and mother, 'you will live a long life, full of blessing.'" (Eph. 6:2-3)

6. **Such a parent guarantees his own child a happy old age.** "Teach your children to choose the right path, and when they are older, they will remain upon it" (Prov.) 22:6.

    We've already dealt with this teaching in the first chapter. And no, this verse doesn't deal specifically with spanking, but it does have to do with teaching and discipline and helping our kids choose the right path for their lives.

7. **The parent who corrects his child may very well save the life of his child.** "Don't fail to correct your children. They won't die if you spank them" (Prov.23:13).

    I used to read that text to say that spanking in itself wouldn't kill a child. They might try to make you think it was going to kill them, but it wouldn't. However, the real point of the verse is that the child who has been properly brought up, including physical discipline, will be less likely to be involved in a brawl, die while driving drunk, or get shot while committing a crime. He or she is also less likely to die of a sexually transmitted disease. In other words, a child who has been disciplined is more likely to live a law-abiding, godly, and thus safer life. There are benefits to proper discipline that reach far beyond the present moment.

8. **The parent who spanks the child keeps him from going to hell.** "Physical discipline may well save them from death" (Prov. 23:14).

    The idea here is of saving them from spiritual death. The word used is "Sheol" which is translated both death and hell. A child who learns to love, respect, and fear his earthly parents is far more likely to love, respect, and fear his heavenly Father. Someone has said, "Everything else in the modern home is controlled with the flick of a switch. Why not the children?" I heartily concur.

Guidelines for Spanking

1. **Begin at an early age.** Spanking, when appropriate, should begin at an early age—as soon as the child is old enough to understand. Proverbs 19:18 says, "Discipline your children while there is hope. If you don't, you will ruin their lives." This proverb obviously implies that we can't wait until it's too late.

2. **Build such a relationship that the worst part of the spanking for the child is the disappointment of the parent.** When I did something deserving of corporal punishment, my mother sent me out into the yard to break a small limb off our wild cherry tree which she would, in turn, use as a switch. But I knew my mother loved me very much; and I loved her very much. So, as much as I hated the punishment itself, it hurt me even more that I had disappointed my mother.

3. **Tell the child what he or she did wrong. Sternly, seriously, but without anger, you should tell the child exactly why he or she is being punished.** Ask the child to tell you what he or she did wrong. Ask the child to state what the punishment will be. And while it may sound like it rings hollow, tell the child that you are doing this because you love him or her.

4. **The spanking should be administered firmly enough to inflict pain.** Some children stubbornly resist showing emotion, so in most cases the spanking should last until the will is broken and the child cries.

5. **Use something other than your hand.** This is certainly not a hard and fast rule, but it is better to use a neutral object so that the punishment is not as directly related to the parent. My father used his hand to spank me, but I can actually only remember one such spanking. I had sassed my mother, and the resulting spanking made a lasting impression. However, my mother used a switch. Some parents use a paddle. The instrument of choice for Jan and me was a wooden spoon, and we called it Woody.

Jan even drew a little face on it, making it more personal. Actually, the threat of Woody ordinarily produced the desired result, especially with Jennifer.

6. **After the spanking, reiterate what the child did wrong and why you spanked him or her.** This should be followed by a hug and the reassurance of your love and your willingness to move on if he is truly sorry.

7. **Parents should always support each other in disciplining the children.** If there are differences of opinion as to the proper approach, they should be aired in private and *never* in front of the child. Unfortunately, there are many kids who grow up with two sets of rules in their homes, their mother's and their father's.

8. **Never spank in front of friends.** The object is not to humiliate but to teach that misbehavior has consequences.

9. **Never discipline in anger.** Biblical discipline is not child abuse. And child abuse should never be justified in the name of biblical discipline. Every precaution should be taken to make sure that a parent is never out of control and that a child is never injured.

10. **Always carry through with promised punishment.** Few things raise my blood pressure faster than being around a misbehaving child and hearing a parent repeat again and again, "If you don't behave, I'm going to spank you. If you don't behave, I'm going to spank you." I've been tempted to say, "Hey, would you like for me to do it for you?" The threat of punishment without the follow through does far more damage than good. It's like getting immunized against a disease, but in this case the child is immunized against any respect or fear whatsoever for the parent. And by the way, this has to be the dumbest question ever asked by a parent: *"Do you want me to spank you?"*

TAKING TIME-OUT

Thus far we've talked mostly about spanking as a form of discipline. However, spanking should be used only as a last resort and even then for only the most serious of misbehaviors. The reason I've devoted so much space to it is simply because it has been under attack and is being largely abandoned even though the Bible specifically calls for it.

There are several other popular forms of discipline that can be effective, and time-outs may be the most effective in most situations, especially for younger children. A time-out is effective because it allows the child to think about what he or she has done, and the Bible certainly affirms the principle of solitude. But there are many other things to commend use of the time-out. It helps keep the parent from overreacting. Furthermore, misbehavior is sometimes the result of emotional exhaustion, especially with preschoolers. Therefore, a time-out gives the child a chance to quiet down and rest up.

The biggest problem with a time-out is that it may not be looked upon as punishment by some kids, especially if they are unsupervised and sent to a room that is full of entertaining books, toys, and electronic media. Actually, our son, Shan, enjoyed being sent to his room unless we took further steps to assure that it was a less-than-pleasant experience. However, Shan and Lise, our daughter-in-law, have continued the tradition, and their four-year-old, Jack, has caught on fast.

When he was only two, Lise and Jack were at a friend's house and when it came time to go and Lise told Jack to get ready, he defiantly said no. Then realizing what he had done and also knowing the drill, he yelled out, "Time-out!" and went over and sat down for his self-imposed sentence. After a few minutes Lise told him his time-out was over. So he got up. But when Lise told him to take her hand and go with her, he again defiantly said no. Realizing the second infraction called for a more severe punishment, he turned his Pampered bottom to his mother and said, "Spank!"

The fact is, children know that punishment for misbehavior is not only right but also that it should be expected. It's a part of that whole security thing I wrote about earlier. As children grow older, taking away possessions, taking away privileges, and taking away freedom—grounding, become the predominant forms of punishment. But the fact is that both moral absolutes and family ground rules must be enforced.

WHAT'S REALLY IMPORTANT

Children certainly need clearly defined limitations if they are to have disciplined behavior. Bedtime, bedtime ritual, homework, family chores, mealtime routine, media limitations, phone privileges, these are all matters of determination for each individual family. But they must be clearly defined for your family and clearly communicated to your family. What about getting up in the morning? What about having friends over? Again, the rules change as the kids get older, but any changes need to be clearly defined as do the consequences for breaking those rules.

My primary advice in this area would be to reserve the absolutes for those things that are really important in your understanding. This becomes more and more important as your kids enter middle school and high school. Don't major on the minors! Don't sweat the small stuff! Don't get so busy fighting minor skirmishes that you end up losing major battles. Being in church when the doors are open was never an option for our kids, nor should it be for yours. However, I can remember the fad of not wearing socks back when Shan was in high school. I insisted that he wear socks. Looking back on that, I'm quite confident that God couldn't have cared less, and it was a silly issue for me as a parent to be concerned about.

I must tell you that I hate body piercings. Earrings for girls look nice. Beyond that, if God had intended for our bodies to be adorned with rings, studs, and chains, He would have provided the extra holes. Furthermore, as a senior pastor, I don't have to employ any guys who show up for work with rings anywhere but on their fingers or around their shirt collars. However, I remember a mother bringing her teenage daughter to me after church and saying, "Pastor John, look at this! Isn't this disgraceful?" Her daughter was wearing a nose ring. Now, I've already staked out my position on body piercing; however, this was a dedicated Christian girl who was being humiliated by her mother. So I called the mother by name and said, "Knowing the sort of girl your daughter is, if this is the worst thing she ever does, you can count yourself as very fortunate." As they walked away the girl turned back toward me and mouthed the words, "Thank you."

We need to recognize that issues like respect for God's authority, governmental authority, and parental authority, honesty, integrity, trustworthiness, and morality are far more substantive than shirttails hanging out, vegetables left on the plate, or wearing socks to church. But some parents understand that and basically abdicate their responsibility as parents in regard to other substantive issues like curfews, associates, and church involvement far too soon. We also tend to forget that God's absolutes include more than just the Ten Commandments. Dr. Rick Fowler wrote an article in *Christian Parenting Today* that provides a list of some of those absolutes. Among them he lists:[4]

- Be kind and forgive others. (Eph. 4:32)
- Treat your body as the Temple of God. 1 Cor.6:19-20)
- Give to God's work. (2 Cor. 9:6-8)
- Children, honor and obey your parents. (Eph. 6:1-3)
- Do not be bound together with unbelievers.(2 Cor. 6:14)
- Respect those in authority. (Rom. 13:1)
- Do not lie to one another. (Col. 3:9)
- Do not use coarse, filthy language. (Eph. 5:4)

Out of those absolutes grow your specific house rules. Unlike those absolutes, house rules tend to change as the kids grow older. For instance, the teaching of 1 Cor. 6 on your body being the temple of the Holy Spirit might relate to bedtime for a five-year-old, but to rules concerning alcohol, tobacco, and drugs for the adolescent.

However, grace is to be more than something we say before eating a meal. Grace can be exhibited toward our kids in some issues that deal more with taste—or lack thereof—and opinions. You may be embarrassed by your kids from time to time, but take heart; they're embarrassed by you too.

STAND FIRM

Once you have discovered the absolutes and determined the house rules, it is time to stand firm. Waffling on the rules only produces confusion in the child, resentment between parents, and excuses for misbehavior. Make sure the punishment fits the crime. Make sure it is age appropriate. And then follow through. The only exception should be when the initial decision was obviously wrong or too severe. I have changed, "You are grounded for the rest of your life," to "You are grounded for the next week." But it should have been the latter in the first place.

When your kids reach their teens, you are on the home stretch as to helping them become the responsible adults God intends for them to be. So while this is a time to give more and more responsibility, it is no time to quit parenting. Our kids were told long before they were interested that they couldn't date until they were 16. It wasn't a big deal to Shan, but Jennifer began testing us many months in advance. The ultimate test came when a freshman in college from our church asked her to be his date for homecoming at his university the weekend before she was to turn sixteen. He was a good kid. It was a daytime date. It would only miss the date we had set by less than a week. But 16 was what we had said, and 16 it was. After all, you only turn 16 once.

Curfews were another area of constant testing. We stood firm on 9:00 P.M. on weeknights, 11:00 P.M. on Fridays, and 10:00 on Saturdays. Weeknights there is school the next day. Fridays there are very few things teenagers can be doing after 11:00 that they should be doing. And the Saturday night curfew honored our faith and affirmed the importance of being fresh for worship on the Lord's Day. Were there ever exceptions? Sure! But each one had to be individually justified.

A FEW REMINDERS

The subject of discipline is a huge one in importance and subject matter. Whole books have been written on the subject; none better than Dr. Dobson's, *Dare to Discipline.* Certainly one chapter in a book cannot come close to exhausting the subject. But I've tried to lay out some important principles, uphold biblical teaching, and debunk some of the politically correct nonsense that is so prevalent in parenting today. So let me close this section with a few important reminders.

Recognize the difference between a careless act and a defiant act. One is to be corrected, and the other to be punished.

Don't discipline in anger. This cannot be overemphasized. While corrective discipline should take place as soon after the misbehavior as possible, disciplining in anger is in itself misbehavior, so give yourself a "time-out" when needed. It is altogether proper to tell your child, "We'll deal with this after dinner," or at some other specified time. It is said that domestic violence is the least reported crime in America. Don't even open the door to being a part of the escalation of child abuse in our country.

Do discipline in love. The old cliché, "This is going to hurt me more than it is going to hurt you," should actually be true. A good parent loves his or her child too much to allow misbehavior to go unchallenged. But that love also must be communicated in words and physical affection.

Communicate, communicate, communicate. Good discipline involves telling your children what they did wrong, why you are correcting them, how you are going to correct them, reaffirming your love as the motivation for the correction, and promising a repeat performance if their behavior does not change.

Be consistent. If there are predetermined punishments for violating the absolutes and the ground rules in your home, make sure they are consistently carried out. Establish boundaries, and then don't back down. If you say you are going to do it, do it. In Ted Tripp's book, *Shepherding a Child's Heart,* he says, "Your children must understand that when you speak for the first time, you have spoken for the last time."[6] It is consistency that develops a value system of right and wrong in the minds and hearts of your children.

Admit when you are wrong. There are times when you blow it as a parent. You make a faulty judgment about your child's behavior, overreact, respond in anger, or discipline them inappropriately. Hey, your kids know they have imperfect parents. So affirm that by telling them you were wrong. I can remember several occasions when I knelt beside by children's beds and apologized for fouling up. When you do, their respect for you only grows.

Praise good behavior. Because of space limitations, we've dealt only with corrective discipline for bad behavior. To discipline means to teach, and we do that as much or more by affirming the good as by correcting the bad. As parents, we should purposely look for good behaviors to praise and reinforce.

Have confidence. You know that establishing limits, rules, and consequences is in your child's best interest. You know it would be easier to be permissive but that true love requires strong parenting. You know that what you are doing is motivated by love. So don't apologize for strong parenting. Have confidence.

Set the example. Children learn right behavior far more by seeing it modeled than by simply hearing it taught. Make sure you're not setting the bar higher for your kids than the one you set for yourself.

Remember, de-parenting is as important as parenting. As your kids grow older you've got to take less responsibility and give them more responsibility. The challenge is in letting go of too much too soon.

Finally, a word to those of you who feel you have already blown it and it's too late to catch up. **It is never too late to start being the parent God has called you to be.** It is certainly easier to start at birth and do everything right—as if anyone ever did. Being firm with older children after having been permissive for years will be difficult at first. There will be resentment. But you can succeed if you follow biblical principles, explain why you are doing what you are doing, and don't back down.

Chapter Six

Teach Values

In *Adolescence Isn't Terminal*, Kevin Leman recounts a newspaper article about Sarah Jessica Parker being practically mobbed outside a Manhattan restaurant by an adoring band of teenaged girls.[1] She and her husband, the actor Matthew Broderick, had just eaten out when they were spotted by all these girls, mostly in their early teens, and they were all gushing, "We love your show!" Even Parker was troubled and reportedly said to her husband, "Matthew, they're too young to watch *Sex and the City*." And, indeed, they were and are. For that matter so are you and I.

I've never watched that show. We didn't have HBO in our home, and if you truly care about teaching values in your home, one positive thing you can do is get rid of HBO and the other premium channels if you have them. *Sex in the City*, typical premium channel fare, was a show starring Parker's character who is a sex columnist for a New York paper. It touches on subjects we're not even going to mention here. She and her friends have the morals of alley cats and live by the philosophy of "If it feels good, do it."

However, according to Kate Betts, editor in chief of *Harper's Bazaar*, Sarah Jessica Parker and her costars now define fashion for the younger set. She writes, "They've become the new fashion authority. The clothes on the show are so sexy, and fashion hasn't been so sexy in a long time. The short skirts, the cocktail look. It's in-your-face and fun."[2] When Parker wore a signature gold ID necklace on one episode, hundreds of girls rushed out to order identical ones. And it would appear that most of the teenaged girls who aren't mimicking Sarah Jessica Parker are trying to imitate Britney Spears with her "slutty is in" approach to fashions.

But my problem is not so much with Parker, Spears, and other popular entertainers. It is not their primary responsibility to set an example for your kids. But I am tremendously troubled and even grieved by the absence of parental responsibility I see exhibited today. Fashion is only one small expression of values, but I can't imagine what some of our parents are thinking in the clothes they allow their kids to wear or not wear even to church.

The blindness of some parents is beyond understanding. Some years ago I called on a church family that I hadn't seen in our worship services for several weeks. The ten-year-old son greeted me at the door and invited me to have a seat in the family room where he had been watching TV while he went and got his dad. When dad joined me he told me they were looking for another church because I talked too much about sex from the pulpit. I'm still trying to figure that one out. What made it ironic was that the movie his son was watching on HBO when I came in was R-rated and filled with nudity and graphic sexuality. Can you imagine that kid's confusion caused by his dad's professed concern along with the contradictory message of what was being allowed in the home?

Values are those rules or guidelines for our lives that we embrace and that not only govern our lives but also influence the fabric of our society as well. While there are certain intrinsic values God has placed within all of His creation, the fact is that most of our values are taught and then embraced. It is the family that provides the primary school of values for our children as well as the testing ground in which those values are proven. Thus, parents who take the time to teach and model moral, ethical, and spiritual standards for their children are rewarded by seeing those children go out into the world with strength of character and values that make them productive members of society, a positive influence on their peers, and most importantly, people who are pleasing to God.

The growing secularization of our society, the banning of God from the public school arena, and the moral slide of society as a whole have all combined to make teaching values more difficult—but all the more imperative. The family is the child's first and most important teacher when it comes to issues of morality and personal virtue. As Christian parents we have the very special privilege of not only conveying our values, but God's values to our children. Actually, more than a privilege, we have the obligation to do so.

TEACHING VALUES

The best model for teaching values is still found in the Old Testament in the passage the Jewish people refer to as the "Shema." It is the Jewish creed that opens synagogue worship and is recited twice a day by devout Jews. Because of its constant reinforcement, it has had a profound affect upon Judaism. Here it is:

> Hear, O Israel! The Lord is our God, the Lord alone. And you must love the Lord your God with all your heart, all your soul, and all your strength. And you must commit yourselves wholeheartedly to these commands I am giving you today. Repeat them again and again to your children. Talk about them when you are at home and when you are away on a journey, when you are lying down and when you are getting up again. Tie them to your hands as a reminder, and wear them on your forehead. Write them on the doorposts of your house and on your gates.
>
> (Deut. 6:4-9)

We teach our children values through our words. When Moses wrote the words found in Deut. 6, the children of Israel had been wandering in the wilderness for 40 years. Now they were preparing to go into the Promised Land. Moses would not be going with them. So there was a sense of urgency in his words. He knew that in the Promised Land his people would encounter all sorts of ungodly things. They would meet people who worshipped pagan gods. He wanted them to remember that the God they worshipped was the true God. He wanted them to stand strong against the pagan influences and he wanted them to teach their children to do the same.

We are not on a journey leading to a physical Promised Land, but we are living in a world that is increasingly hostile toward God and godliness. And while we may not be tempted by graven images, I want to remind you that idolatry is not limited to gods of wood and stone. An idol is anything that takes your primary allegiance away from the true God, that drains your devotion and allegiance from God, who is deserving, and squanders it on those pursuits or things that are far less worthy.

Let me ask you this probing question. What have you talked about with your family this past week? Chances are you have talked about work, about school, about friends, about the weather, about the ballgame, about money. But have God and the things of God been major matters of discussion around your house this week? What did your children hear you talking about to others? Kids are quick to pick up on what is really important to us. They are learning from our conversations what their priorities, ambitions, dreams, and values should be. Woodrow Wilson said in an address way back in 1904, "If you wish your children to be Christians, you must really take the trouble to be Christians yourselves."

As much as I am grieved by the removal of prayer and Bible reading from our public schools; as much as I realize that a truly secular public square is one without morality or values; and as much as I am alarmed by the diminishing impact of the church in America; the fact is that Christian education is not the business of the public schools or of the government. And while the church is in the Christian education business, the limitations of time allow it only a relatively small influence in the lives of your children. What is taught at church a few hours a week can in no way compare to the influence of what is taught in your home. I'm not minimizing the importance of the church or the Christian school, but I am saying Christian parents cannot use them as an escape from the personal responsibility to teach their children.

The Hebrews were very successful in making their faith an integral part of their lives. The reason is that their religious education was practical, life-oriented, and used the ebb and flow of the teachable moments in their children's lives. They simply used the context of everyday life to teach their children about God. If you want your children to embrace godly values you must teach them in the everyday experiences of life. However, the words we speak are not the most important conveyer of values.

We teach our children through our actions. Kids mirror their parents. They reflect our attitudes, prejudices, convictions, standards, and values. Even poor parenting skills are passed on from generation to generation unless someone intentionally interrupts the cycle. It is amazing how drug and alcohol abuse are so often passed on from generation to generation. So again, modeling is a powerful force in parenting, for the good or for the bad.

What do your children see in your life? What values are you demonstrating to them? Is your faith in Christ clear to them? Is your commitment to Christ authentic? What about your love for and faithfulness to your spouse? What kind of language do your kids hear at home? It is amazing how many parents punish their children for the very behaviors they are modeling.

Actions do speak louder than words. Although what we say is of tremendous importance, how we live makes an even greater impact on our children. Do you remember that great television commercial of several years ago? It shows a series of events in which the actions of a young boy mirror those of his father. The father washed the car and so the son picked up a sponge to help him. The father painted the fence, so the little boy grabbed a brush and dipped it in the paint can too. The father lit a cigarette, so his son reached for one too. He wanted to be just like Dad. And then the commercial faded to black.

Our children are watching us. They are determining their values in large part by the values they see us living out. What we do, they assume to be the right thing. Again, it is what we do more than what we say. If we teach one thing with our mouths but appear to contradict that teaching with our behavior, they are far more likely to believe the latter. This may be especially true in matters of faith. It is easy for us to confess truths that we hold dear, but a disparity between what we profess and what we practice will give our children plenty of reason to question what we profess. A.W. Tozer put it this way, "An intelligent observer of our human scene who heard the Sunday morning sermon and later watched the Sunday afternoon conduct of those who heard it would conclude that he had been examining two distinct and contrary religions."[3]

By the way, our children quickly pick up on the inconsistency between parents who criticize removal of prayer and Bible reading from the public schools and the lack of prayer and Bible reading at home. They are puzzled by the parent who is critical of the erosion of the right of Christians to speak out yet does not proclaim Christ when opportunities present themselves. I can assure you that telling kids "Do as I say, not as I do," is an exercise in futility. Ritch Grimes says that has as much influence as throwing a piece of meat into a tank of piranhas and telling them not to eat it. The piranhas are going to do what comes naturally. Our kids are going to do what comes natural and respond to what they see more than what they hear.[4]

Purdue University conducted a study of how teens develop their religious beliefs.[5] Of those students participating in the study, just over half read the Bible on a regular basis and nearly seventy-five percent said they pray regularly. Obviously there had been a significant adoption of values from parents, but how did that come about? Well, talking about faith was important. There were 53 percent who agreed that their fathers had taught them to pray and 67 percent said their mothers had done likewise. Nearly two-thirds said their fathers had talked to them about their religious beliefs with about the same percentage of mothers. Between 93 and 95 percent said they were encouraged by one or both of their parents to regularly attend church.

However, in the Purdue study, modeling was pointed to as an even more important factor in the development of the beliefs of those participating in the study than was instruction of verbal encouragement. Researchers discovered three specific points of transference of values: kids having discussions with their parents, kids participating in joint activities with their parents, and kids observing what their parents did. Notice that two of the three points have to do with actions rather than words.

Actually, the weaving together of words and actions is what has the most powerful impact on children. The best approach for parents to take in teaching values to their children is to instruct their children in regard to a value, discuss it from a biblical perspective, and then engage in an activity in which that value is embraced. The Purdue study showed that the degree to which parents used multiple approaches in teaching their children about their beliefs and modeled participation in activities related to those beliefs determined how accurately young adults understood what their parents believed and embraced it themselves.

A story from *Guideposts* underscores the importance of consistency between our words and actions.

> The cold Iowa dawn was still an hour off, but already Dad and I had finished a big job on our farm. We'd loaded 100 head of cattle for market into two waiting semi-trailers. I was 16 and this was the first time I'd seen the cattle off to market. Dad had made it my job to keep the feeder full with the right mix. I'd seen them come in as scrawny yearlings and fatten up to 1,100 pounds a piece. The price was right and it was time to sell. There was just the paperwork to complete.
>
> "Got to have your John Hancock right there," said Mick, one of the drivers, as he handed Dad the clipboard.
>
> "What's this, Mick?" asked Dad.
>
> "Something that Uncle Sam wants you to sign. Says you kept the cattle off Stibestrol for two weeks before the slaughter."
>
> "I felt the blood rush to my head. Stibestrol was used as a feed additive to promote growth. We'd debated its use and had gone ahead. The government had changed its regulations several times, and the form Mick had was new. I'd been giving the cattle Stibestrol all along.
>
> "I don't think it makes a whole lot of difference myself," said Mick. "Don't see how they can tell anyway."
>
> Dad scratched the ground with his boot. We'd be the laughing stock of the county if we unloaded our cattle because of some silly government regulation. Another two weeks and the market price would be sure to fall. Finally Dad looked up.
>
> "Better unload 'em," he said. That was 15 autumns ago and I'm a farmer myself now. Dad died a few years back. But his example lives on for me. That morning as the cattle came back down the chutes and

the daylight stretched across the horizon, Dad didn't say anything. He didn't have to. Honesty wasn't just a value Dad talked about. It was something that he lived."[6]

Our children are watching our lives to figure out what is really important in life. What are we teaching them? What lessons are they learning from us? Would you be pleased for your children to embrace all the values you live out in your personal life from day to day?

VALUES WE SHOULD TEACH

Toward the end of her career, it seems to me that Ann Landers went the way of society as a whole. However, even in the later years she sometimes gave a winner of an answer. Ralph from Oakland, California wrote, "This is for the woman who was distressed about her son. I would like to ask her some questions about the boy. Is he disrespectful? Has he been arrested for drunk driving? Has he been kicked out of college for cheating? Has he made his girlfriend pregnant? Does he get failing grades? Does he steal money from your purse? If you can answer no to all these questions, stop complaining. You have a great kid." But Ann wrote back that the letter showed just how much times have changed in that if a kid isn't on drugs, getting failing grades, hasn't been arrested for drunk driving, or kicked out of college, hasn't made his girlfriend pregnant, or stolen from someone's purse that he's now considered a great kid. But Ann made the point that Ralph says nothing of achievement, integrity, responsibility, decency, morality, or service. She rightly observed that this was a sad commentary on our times and lamented the direction our nation is headed.

So in a society that has largely forsaken its values, where do we begin? What are the values we should be most careful to impart? Obviously, whole books can and have been written in answer to those very questions. For instance, Jim and Elizabeth George have written *God's Wisdom for Little Boys,* sub-titled, *Character-Building Fun from Proverbs*, and *God's Wisdom for Little Girls* with the same sub-title. These are values-oriented books for preschoolers and early elementary aged children. Similar books are available for older elementary students and adolescents. But let me at least mention seventeen specific values I believe we need to be teaching our sons and daughters.

1. **Value God as the Creator**

   The world teaches children that we are merely cosmic accidents, that we are simply the highest progression to date on the evolutionary tree. Not only is evolution itself more and more untenable from a scientific standpoint, but when you dismiss the teachings of Genesis you take away the foundation of most every Christian doctrine: sin, the fall, death, sacrifice, salvation, and much, much more. Contact Answers in Genesis for some wonderful teaching materials on God as Creator[7] or check out your local Christian bookstore.

   It was only when I was confronted with the implications of evolution when I was a pre-med major at a state university that I really began looking for answers, answers that led me to an uncompromised faith in the Lord and the teachings of His Word.

   It takes far more faith to believe that our world came about by accident than it does to take God at His Word, "In the beginning God created the heavens and the earth" (Gen. 1:1). Parents, you have your work cut out for you, but stand your ground in valuing God as Creator.

2. **Value the Creation**

   The Bible says, "The earth is the Lord's and everything in it" (Ps. 24:1). Many times Bible-believing Christians seem to ignore the teaching of Gen. 1:28 where mankind was told, "Multiply and fill the earth and subdue it. Be masters over the fish and birds and all the animals." Everything was created for man's benefit, but man also has the responsibility to take care of creation.

3. **Value People**

   The whole of Ps. 24:1 reads, "The earth is the Lord's and everything in it. The world and all its people belong to Him." Furthermore, Gen. 1:26 tells us that God made people in His own image, He patterned them after himself.

Our children need to learn that every man, woman, boy, and girl has tremendous worth in the eyes of God no matter who they are, what they've done, the color of their skin, or from what country they come.

4. **Value the Word of God**
   One of the things my parents did for which I will be eternally grateful is that they taught me to value the Bible as the very Word of God. Every child needs to understand from the time they are able to understand anything that, "All Scripture is inspired by God and is useful to teach us what is true and to make us realize what is wrong in our lives. It straightens us out and teaches us what is right. It is God's way of preparing us in every way, fully equipped for every good thing God wants us to do" (2 Tim. 3:16-17). Valuing the Word of God gives us a basis on which to determine the legitimacy of other values.

5. **Value the Family**
   In this day and age, when the family is under attack more than ever before, it is of greater importance than ever that we teach our children the sacredness of marriage, that marriage is between a man and a woman (Gen. 2:24, Matt. 19:5, Eph. 5:31), and that children are a gift from God. Don't compromise the value of marriage or family.

6. **Value the Church**
   Because the church is made up of imperfect people, the church is imperfect in that sense. But beware of being critical of the church in the presence of your children. They need to value it as the Body of Christ and the Bride of Christ. They need to be drawn to it, not alienated from it. Remember, Christ gave His life for the church (Eph. 5:25).

7. **Value the Government**
   We are to value the government not because it is always right or because we like its officials, but because civil government is of God. Romans 13:1-2 reads, "Obey the government, for God is the One

who put it there. All governments have been placed in power by God. So those who refuse to obey the laws of the land are refusing to obey God." Our children need to see that without civil government there would be anarchy and chaos. Government was designed by God for our good, so value the government.

8. **Value Wholesome Speech**
Paul writes in Eph. 4:29 (NASB), "Let no unwholesome word proceed from your mouth, but only such a word as is good for edification according to the need of the moment, that it may give grace to those who hear." I believe that the prevalence of foul language in most every aspect of daily life today is a strong contributor to the growing incivility, lack of respect, and ungodly behavior that is sweeping across our land. Teach your children well to abstain from crude, vulgar, or profane language. My mother washed my mouth out with soap only once. That's all it took.

9. **Value Life**
We must teach by example the honor and dignity of all people and instill in our children compassion, sensitivity, and kindness. We do this by helping the poor, protecting the unborn, visiting prisoners, and caring for the aged.

10. **Value Human Sexuality**
Raise your son to be a one-woman man and your daughter to be a one-man woman. Teach your children to save sexual intimacy for marriage and teach them why. (See Josh McDowell's *Why True Love Waits*[8]). Have zero tolerance for pornography. Help them understand scriptures such as 2 Tim. 2:22, "Run from anything that stimulates youthful lust. Follow anything that makes you want to do right," and 1 Thess. 4:3, "God wants you to be holy, so you should keep clear of all sexual sin."

11. **Value Masculinity and Femininity**
There has been a campaign on for a generation, whether intentional or unintentional, to feminize the American male. There is

constant assault on gender distinctive. There is even a new word, *metrosexual,* to identify "men who are in touch with their feminine side." But God made us male and female. Fathers need to teach their sons what it means to be masculine and mothers must teach their daughters what it means to be feminine. Gordon Dalbey writes, "The church has done much over the centuries to encourage men to pursue feminine virtues. But we have not sought and portrayed Christ-centered ways to pursue masculine virtues. It is not enough for Christians to portray weakness and tenderness as acceptable in a man. We also must portray the manly strength and firmness that is of God. We must demonstrate that weakness confessed and submitted to the Living God through Jesus Christ ultimately brings the very masculine strength for which men hunger: toughness in the face of opposition, decisiveness in the face of uncertainty, and saving power in the face of danger."[9]

12. Value Private Property

While sharing is a biblical value and should be encouraged, so should respecting the private property of others. Theft, covetousness, discontent, and jealousy are all condemned in Scripture.

13. Value Honesty

This is a building block not only of character, but also of healthy family life. Dishonesty, deception, and so-called white lies should not be tolerated. And honesty, even more than some other values, is one that your child will quickly recognize as either being modeled by you or not modeled by you. It's pretty difficult to teach your child the value of honesty when you lie about his or her age to get a cheaper admission to the amusement park or a cheaper meal at the restaurant.

14. Value Gratitude

When we teach our children to be grateful for what they have and content to live without what they don't have, we guard them from the destructive influence of covetousness. Gratitude not only guards them from the negative but is a positive building block in their relationship with God and with their fellow man.

15. Value Passionate Living

Contentment and wanting to be and do all God intended for us to be and do are not in contradiction. Passion is sometimes called soul hunger, a burning desire to achieve or fulfill a mission. There are many things about our society that tend to devalue passion. But advancements in society are most often made by people who refuse to accept the status quo, refuse to just get by, and instead choose to live life to the hilt. Fred Hartley, in his book *Parenting at Its Best*, has written, "Passion is the smile on the face of a challenge, a gleam in the eye of mission, a bounce in the stride of opportunity, adrenaline in the bloodstream of purpose."[10] I like that. Teach your child to value passionate living.

16. Value Vision

Teach your children early in life the value of goal-setting, of seeing what they want to achieve and mapping out a strategy to achieve it. That can range from helping a preschooler save his pennies in order to purchase a desired toy for himself to college-related goals for your high school student and determining what it will demand of him to get into the school of his choice. Goals should be SMART: Specific, Measurable, Achievable, Realistic, and Time-specific. Teaching such value to your children is key to developing visionary leaders for the future.

17. Value Wisdom

John MacArthur has a tremendous chapter in his book, *What the Bible Says About Parenting*, on "Teaching Your Children," in which he presents the Book of Proverbs as the Holy Spirit-inspired summation of wisdom. Thus Proverbs becomes the perfect textbook for parents to teach their children the value of practical wisdom. Through the Book of Proverbs you can:

Teach your children to fear God   (1:7, 9:10)
Teach your children to guard their minds   (4:23, 23:7)
Teach your children to obey their parents   (1:8, 4:1-4, 6:20-23)
Teach your children to carefully select their companions
                                        (1:10, 1:11-18, 2:10-15 13:20)

Teach your children to control their lusts
                    (2:16-19, 5:3-5, 6:23-33, 7:6-27)
Teach your children to enjoy their spouses   (5:15, 18-20)
Teach your children to watch their words
                    (4:24, 10:11, 12:18, 22)
Teach your children to pursue their work
                    (6:6-11, 10:4-5, 22:29)
Teach your children to manage their money
                    (3:9-10, 11:24-26, 15:27, 22:16)
Teach your children to love their neighbors (3:27-29, 25:21-22)

So you already have the greatest book that has ever existed on teaching your children the value of wisdom.

There are many other values that we need to teach our children. We've not even mentioned the value of sobriety. Even as I write, the newspapers are filled with several stories of the tragic deaths of teens related to alcohol and drugs. But again, if your example is not consistent with what you teach, your children are most likely going to do as you do and not as you say. We've not looked at the value of generosity, or selfless love, or a hundred other values that would be worth our consideration. In other words, teaching values is a full-time job. That's why Moses wrote, "Repeat them again and again to your children. Talk about them when you are at home and when you are away on a journey, when you are lying down and when you are getting up again" (Deut. 6:7).

REINFORCING THOSE VALUES

Earlier in this chapter we discussed the two primary methods of teaching values. We teach values by our words and by our actions. We reinforce those values through our continued words and our continuing actions. In other words, parenting is an endless job.

However, before we close this seemingly endless chapter, let me give you six very simple, practical reinforcements of the Christian values we've been talking about.

1. **Make sure you are totally committed to Christ yourself.** Kids are quick to spot a phony. So make sure your commitment is more than

a surface thing. Work on deepening your walk with the Lord. Make sure you love God with all your heart, soul, mind, and strength.

2. **Continually nurture a loving relationship with your children.** Josh McDowell says, "Rules without a relationship lead to rebellion." Unless your kids know that the values you teach and the rules you uphold are grounded in your unconditional love for them, they will see those things as obstacles to overcome rather than guidelines to live by.

3. **Make sure your kids are into the Word of God.** It is important they understand that the values we talk about aren't just Mom's and Dad's, but they are rooted and grounded in what God says. Remember Deut. 6 when Moses told the Jewish people to tie God's commands to their hands and wear them on their foreheads and write them on the doorposts and gates of their houses. We ought to saturate our children in the Word of God. One of the best things my mother ever did for me was to teach me to memorize scripture even before I was old enough to read.

4. **Minimize their exposure to the negative influences of the world.** Later I'll devote a whole chapter to controlling the media in your home. Every mother in the animal kingdom has the natural instinct to protect her young. How tragic that human parents sometimes ignore that very instinct when it comes to protecting children from the evil influences that surround them.

5. **Show respect for the church.** Parents, the church is the best ally you have in raising "G-Rated" kids. Your kids know the church and the pastors aren't perfect, but you need to be careful about exposing your children to your own criticisms and thus causing them to lose respect for the very people you need to help you in raising your children to be who God intended them to be. Be quick to commend the church and very slow to criticize.

6. **Pray for your children and with your children on a regular basis.** Pray about every aspect of their lives—their values, character,

health, strength, and wisdom. Pray for protection, not just physically but also spiritually. Pray for God to bring the right kind of friends into their lives. Pray every day that God will lead them to the right person to marry so that their marriages will be happy and will last their lifetimes. And pray for their spouses, even though you don't yet know who they are.

The following piece has been making the rounds for years. While its author is now unknown, the spiritual wisdom in it demands that it is reprinted. It's entitled, "From Parent to Child."

I gave you life, but I cannot live it for you.
I can teach you things, but I cannot make you learn.
I can give you directions, but I cannot be there to lead you.
I can allow you freedom, but I cannot account for it.
I can take you to church, but I cannot make you believe.
I can teach you right from wrong, but I cannot always decide for you.
I can buy you beautiful clothes, but I cannot make you beautiful inside.
I can offer you advice, but I cannot accept it for you.
I can give you love, but I cannot force it upon you.
I can teach you to share, but I cannot make you unselfish.
I can teach you respect, but I cannot force you to show honor.
I can advise you about friends, but I cannot choose them for you.
I can advise you about sex, but I cannot keep you pure.
I can tell you about lofty goals, but I cannot achieve them for you.
I can teach you about kindness, but I cannot force you to be gracious.
I can warn you about sin, but I cannot make you moral.
I can love you as a child, but I cannot place you in God's family.
I can pray for you, but I cannot make you walk with God.
I can teach you about Jesus, but I cannot make Jesus your Lord.
I can tell you how to live, but I cannot give you eternal life.
There are many things we can't do. Let's make sure we do what we can in teaching values to our children.

Chapter Seven

Set Boundaries

We live in a frightening world. Anyone who loves the Lord and cares anything about biblical morality can easily see that our culture as a whole is rapidly disintegrating morally, ethically, and spiritually. The values now embraced by our society as a whole are mostly at odds with God's divine order of things.

Society is full of frightening trends, including the rejection of absolute truth by which right and wrong is determined and the erosion of the home as the cornerstone institution of our society. Soaring divorce rates, the court-sanctioned practice of abortion, radical feminism, the increase of adultery, the so-called "children's rights" movement, the acceptance of homosexuality, the push for homosexual marriage, the normalization of the single-parent home, and the decline of the nuclear family, all make the age in which we live the most challenging ever in which to raise our kids. Nowhere is that challenge greater than in helping our kids remain sexually pure. Today's teens have to deal with all these issues just at the time they are going through hormonal surges and have emerging feelings that are confusing enough under the best of circumstances.

Pop music pushes casual sex. The Internet, with its pop-up windows, beckons web surfers to explore erotic sites. The fashion world touts midriff-baring designs that sexualize our young women and erotically appeal to our young men and older men as well. Kids often go home to unsupervised surroundings. Young people are having sex at younger ages than ever before. Score-keeping bands of boys make a game out of claiming as many young virgins as possible. And peer pressure says to young girls that if they say no they're a tease and if they say yes they're a slut. But being sexually active is so prevalent in today's teen culture that it is just assumed to be a form of self-expression.

All of this simply underscores the importance of this chapter. I know that those of you with younger children may believe this chapter is irrelevant to you. But I can assure you that even if you do not yet have children it is not too early to determine what you are going to do about this issue of setting boundaries in regard to boy-girl relationships. Furthermore, many of the principles contained in this chapter must be put into place early in a child's life for maximum effectiveness.

By the way, in case I don't yet have your attention, a study reported in the March/April 2003 *Christian Reader*, reports that while there has been a recent decrease both in teen sex and teen pregnancy (it's amazing how the two go together), that 39.9 percent of boys and 37.3 percent of girls in the seventh through twelfth grades are sexually active (by definition, having intercourse), and 20 percent of sexually active girls ages 15 to 19 still get pregnant each year. There is also a significant rise in sexually transmitted diseases among this age group. What increases the scope of the problem significantly is the fact that oral sex is not even included in the above stated statistics. Studies have shown that due to the exposure it has received in the media in recent years, teens don't classify having oral sex as being sexually active, and so they're experimenting more and more with that practice.

START EARLY

We get very concerned about setting boy/girl boundaries when our kids reach adolescence. But if we have not been laying groundwork for healthy sexuality throughout their earlier years, we've probably already lost the battle when our kids become teens.

Begin talking very naturally about sexuality when your children are young and it will allow you to deal with their normal sexual curiosity in a healthy, non-condemning way. It will, however, make you both more approachable and more able to initiate needed conversations when the time comes.

Find books that appropriately display what the human body looks like and talk to your children unashamedly about how God made us male and female. By the time your children are five or six they should know that sex is a wonderful gift expressed *between a husband and a wife*. The thought that anything sexual would ever take place outside the relationship of marriage should sound odd at the very least.

Not all that many years ago parents took pride in protecting their children from growing up too fast. They were allowed to "be children." Competitiveness in every arena children experienced was much more low-key, but especially in the social arena of boy/girl relationships. That was before we put makeup on little girls, gave them training bras years before they had anything to go in them, and dressed them provocatively.

As a consequence, talking to our kids about subjects that were at one time reserved for much later now has to take place earlier. Parent-led sex education is now absolutely essential from early grade school at the latest—not to encourage children to become sexually active but to alert them to the hazards that await them if they venture outside the boundaries you give them. Developmentally, by the age of two, children recognize the differences between boys and girls. By the age of four, most children are interested in babies and the whole birth process.

ANSWER SIMPLY

We've all heard the story about Tommy rushing into the house and asking his mother, "Mom, where did I come from?" She knew this day would come and she was ready. She sat him down and gave him the whole nine yards about the birds and the bees, complete with diagrams and pictures. Proud of herself for responding so well she asked Tommy if she had adequately answered his question. Tommy responded, "Not really, Mom. My friend Billy said he and his family were from Toledo and I just wanted to know where I was from. "

We need to think about age appropriateness and what the child is really asking. We can do as much damage by giving a child too much too early as by failing to discuss what we really need to discuss. In answering questions, answer simply, covering only the basics, and then ask, "Does that explain it?" Then add, "If you want to know more, just ask." Always leave the door open for further discussion.

FRAME SEX POSITIVELY

Because we want to make sure our kids don't get involved in premarital sex, parents often frame sexuality as a bad thing, something to be avoided at all costs. Such an upbringing has had serious repercussions for many Christian couples who come to their wedding night having been taught that sex is something dirty. Actually we should affirm sex as a gift from God, and not just for procreation. Human sexuality is the closest of interpersonal relationships, a marvelous way of showing love, and something intended to bring the heights of pleasure. However, all of that is to be accomplished within the bonds of marriage.

USE TEACHABLE MOMENTS

Today's children are forced to face at an early age issues that most parents didn't deal with until later in life. As a child, I wasn't confronted with homosexuality, abortion, or rape. I assure you that discussions of oral sex or masturbation were not common around our dinner table. However, today your kids may come home with questions about just such issues, even early in elementary school. Such occasions should not be time for dumping too much information, but should be times in which the questions are answered and not avoided.

I remember the questions my young son asked when a family member got pregnant out of wedlock. This was a time not only for teaching about "the facts of life," but even more importantly of showing him how God's way is always the best and how when we violate God's standards there is hurt, pain, and disappointment. Children need to know that the instructions of God's Word are not for the purpose of taking away our enjoyment, but of protecting us because God loves us so much.

INITIATE DISCUSSIONS

It is certainly good for a parent to initiate conversations about sex from time to time, especially with your teen, if for no other reason than to let them know you are comfortable with the subject—whether you are or not—and that they really can talk to you about anything. There were so many things I needed to know that I could have and should have learned from my parents. But here is the sum total of the teaching I received at home. I was heading out the door to go on a date. My mother called me back and said, "Son, always remember to treat the girl you are dating the way you would want another boy to treat the girl you are going to marry." That was it! I'm not exaggerating.

My father and I never had "the talk." And my mother's efforts were limited to that one sentence. Oh, I know, part of it was the time in which I grew up. Other parents didn't do much better. But how sad that I received most of my sex education and lessons about interacting with the opposite sex from other kids who were as ignorant as I was. The misinformation I received and gave would make for a hilarious book.

Some of the best discussions I ever had with my kids on any number of subjects were in the car. Defenses come down. Conversation is more casual. And especially when you are talking about sensitive subjects, you don't have to look at each other. When Dad is talking to his daughter about sex, it's nice to be required to keep your eyes on the road and on the semi that's blasting past you on the Interstate. And quite honestly, as Kevin Leman says in his book, *Adolescence Isn't Terminal,* "Your fourteen-year-old daughter, just a few years into her training bra, loves the fact that she can look out the passenger window of the car, rolling her eyes and thinking to herself, 'I can't believe I'm having this conversation with my dad.'"[1] Initiating a significant conversation with your kids while driving the car is a wonderful tool. But however you do it, do it.

GIVE CORRECT INFORMATION

When you have those conversations don't use slang or try to be cute. Call intercourse "intercourse." Call body parts and bodily functions by their correct names. It always cracks me up when I go to my doctor for a physical and he tells me to go "pee" in a cup. He's a good doctor, but when he says that I feel like I'm dealing with a junior higher.

By the way, teaching our kids about sex should involve both Mom and Dad for both son and daughter. There are some things only a dad can truly explain to his daughter and other things only a mother can truly explain to her son. A daughter needs to hear from her father about how boys and men are stimulated by sight and how that should impact the way she dresses and presents herself. And only a mother can truly explain to her son how a woman thinks and feels, and how her body reacts and responds.

Again, don't give more information than is age appropriate. But whatever information you present, make sure it is correct. Let your kids know they can depend on you to shoot straight with them.

GIVE YOUR KIDS REASONS TO WAIT FOR MARRIAGE

In his book, *How to Save Your Kids from Ruin*, Jerry Johnston gives what he calls, "The Advantages of Abstinence."[2] Let me list them along with a brief word of explanation.

Advantage 1: Avoid sexually transmitted disease.
Abstinence is the only way to guarantee complete protection from such potentially lethal diseases. One in four sexually active teens will contract an STD. Condoms, which fail one out of six times even when kept intact, do not guarantee protection against either STDs or pregnancy.

Advantage 2: Avoid suicidal thoughts and depression.
Studies show a greater incidence of suicidal thoughts among sexually active teens, and they are more likely to have drug and alcohol problems as well.

Advantage 3: Avoid unwanted, ill-timed pregnancy.
Getting pregnant is great when you are married, but it can cause devastating problems for a young girl and her boyfriend as well as for the child.

Advantage 4: Realize the honor of marriage.

Sexual activity before marriage dishonors and undermines marriage.

Advantage 5: Avoid the emotional scars of being used.

For many guys, sex is viewed as a conquest. For most girls, it is a commitment. When the guy gets what he wants he's off to another conquest, leaving the girl with the pain of feeling used. There is never any regret for waiting for the right person at the right time, your wedding night.

Advantage 6: Experience the thrill of sex as it was created.

The Song of Solomon speaks of the supercharged ecstasy of physical love as it was intended by God in marriage.

Advantage 7: Experience long-term love.

Genuine love is quite different from the erotica we see in the media. The best God has for us is found in a long-term relationship encircled with love.

Advantage 8: Your prize of virginity.

Don't give it to anyone except the mate God has prepared just for you. Perhaps the best resource other than the Bible on this subject is *Why True Love Waits* by Josh McDowell. That is not only the name of his book but of a national campaign in which millions of kids have dedicated themselves to living pure, chaste lives. There are ten "Behavior Guidelines" that govern this program for teens:

1. I will date only Christian guys or gals.
2. I will seek my parent's counsel for consenting to date another person.
3. I will understand my standards before I agree to date.
4. I will either plan out or be sure that each date is planned out.
5. I will not put myself or my date in a position to defend his or her right to be pure.

6. I will build up the spiritual, intellectual, and emotional before the physical.
7. I will not be left alone at home with my dating partner.
8. I will not engage in petting or intimate physical contact.
9. I will not lie down with my dating partner.
10. I will not engage in premarital sex.

Mom and Dad, it is your responsibility to provide your children with the ammunition they need to combat the extraordinary forces that are going to try to destroy them down to the world's level and destroy the prize of their virginity. Don't fail them.

COMMUNICATE GOD'S STANDARDS

There is no question that God planned sex for within the context of marriage. Don't be embarrassed to tell your kids that God invented sex as something beautiful and pleasurable but to be enjoyed within the boundary of a total marital commitment. Proverbs 5:18-19 says, "Let your wife be a fountain of blessing for you. Rejoice in the wife of your youth. She is a loving doe, a graceful deer. Let her breasts satisfy you always. May you always be captivated by her love." That's God speaking.

Among other biblical issues you can discuss with your kids, tell them that God created sex (Gen. 2:18-22); God has a plan for sex (Matt. 19:4-6, Gen. 2:24); that God gives instructions on sexuality (Heb. 13:4, 1 Cor. 6:18-20); and God has reasons for you to wait (Deut. 10:12-13, Jer. 29:11). Although there are many reasons for premarital abstinence, the most significant of all is that it is God's will.

GIVE DATING GUIDELINES

Remember my mother's one-sentence sex-education and dating guidelines discussion? "Son always remember to treat the girl you are dating the way you would want another boy to treat the girl you are going to marry." That instruction was woefully inadequate, but it was a great guideline nonetheless. Kids should always be taught to treat the person they are dating with respect.

Another general guideline is that our kids should be careful to not unnecessarily arouse their own sexual feelings or those of their dates. Kids need to watch where they go and be careful as to what they do. If a couple were watching a sexually explicit R-rated movie from the backseat of a car in the drive-in, it would take miraculous intervention to keep them from crossing lines they shouldn't cross.

Aside from such guidelines, however, parents need to put together their own list of specific guidelines for their kids when they begin to date; and then, for goodness sake, enforce them! With that in mind let me give you...

THE CALDWELL DATING RULES

1. You will not date until you are sixteen.
2. When you begin dating you will go out with several different people.
3. You will be home by 11:00 on Friday night and 10:00 on Saturday night.
4. No one of the opposite sex is allowed in the house unless Mom or Dad is home.
5. You will not go anywhere that there is drinking taking place.
6. You will not attend or rent R-rated movies.
7. You will call if you must be late.
8. Always treat the other person with respect.

Were these rules absolutes? Yes, with the exception of curfews, which were adjustable on exceptional, special occasions. Frankly, I didn't have a curfew, and there was nothing I ever did after 11:00 that I ought to have been doing. The 10:00 P.M. curfew on Saturday was because we value church attendance and worship at our house. Part of preparation for effective worship is adequate rest. By the way, none of these rules destroyed or even dented our children's social lives.

IN CONCLUSION

The day in which we live is not only the most challenging ever for parents, it is the most challenging ever for our kids. They need all the help they can get. The very least you can do is provide boundaries for them in areas where they most need help. "But what if they complain? What if they don't like it?" Give me a break! They wouldn't be kids if they didn't object. But providing boundaries gives your kids security and an assurance of your love that far exceeds all the material gifts you can throw at them. So don't apologize for loving your kids enough to set boundaries and ask questions.

You should insist on meeting all your teen's friends. You should expect to know where they are going and when they will be home. Their computer should be accessible to you, including viewing their browser history for the sites they are visiting. Family time should be mandatory, not optional. You should enlist the help of teachers, youth pastors, youth coaches, and parents of friends. You need a network of caring people to help you keep tabs on your kids, although some privacy should be respected. I also agree with what Dr. Donald W. Welch of MidAmerican Nazarene University says, "When a child becomes exclusive, parents should become intrusive." Care enough to take the heat. "Mom, Dad, you don't trust me." "You're right. We love you and we believe in you; but we understand the tremendous temptations you face, and we're going to do everything in our power to help you make the right choices."[3]

SOME RESOURCES TO HELP:

Boy Meets Girl by Josh Harris
Every Young Man's Battle by Stephen Arterburn and Fred Stoeker
I Kissed Dating Goodbye by Josh Harris
Keeping Your Kids Sexually Pure by La Verne Tolbert
Real Teens by George Barna
Sex According to God by Kay Arthur
Talking to Your Kids About Sex by Mark Laaser
Why True Love Waits by Josh McDowell

Chapter Eight

Control the Media

I will be forever thankful that I grew up in the 1950s. It is more than personal nostalgia that makes me wish your kids could grow up in as wholesome and nonthreatening an age as that was. Oh, yes, there was the cold war, the Soviet nuclear threat, and the bomb shelters. But frankly, the threats we endured were obvious and overt rather than insidious and cloaked in societal acceptance.

From a media standpoint, my early years were spent listening to the radio. Every evening I settled in by the big console radio to listen to *The Lone Ranger* ("Hi-Ho Silver...") and *Sergeant Preston* ("On King, on you huskies..."). Right was right, and wrong was wrong. The bad guys always got caught, and the good guys always won out in the end. We got our first TV when I was nine. With a huge antenna on top of our house in Springfield, Missouri, we could pull in two very snowy channels. One was from St. Louis, and the other was from Kansas City. The first television show I ever saw was *The Big Top*, a circus show sponsored by Sealtest Ice Cream. We didn't have *Sesame Street*, but we did have *Howdy Doody*. Furthermore, television was on only from late afternoon until bedtime.

By the time we had a local television station, *I Love Lucy* was the most popular show on TV. Even though Ricky and Lucy were married in real life as well as on TV, any glimpse of their bedroom revealed twin beds; and when Lucy was pregnant in real life she had to be pregnant on the show. But saying the word "pregnant" on television produced a mini-furor. My how times have changed.

Movies for us as a family were an unusual treat. When we did go it was usually to a western like *Red River Valley*. However, every Saturday, the Colonial Bakery sponsored free movies for kids at the Fox Theater on the square in downtown Springfield. My buddies and I rode the city bus downtown, something that was still safe for nine- or ten-year-old kids back then, and enjoyed a full morning of entertainment. Again, more often than not, the feature was a western. There were newsreels, cartoons, and serial movies as well. George Earle was the KWTO radio personality host of the free movies. He and his hand puppet, Polly the Parrot, interviewed kids and entertained between movies. Can you imagine today's kids "tolerating" that? But for us it was tremendous fun and good, clean, wholesome entertainment.

When it came to music, most kids didn't get into that until high school. Like other kids, I had quite a stack of 45s. There was Pat Boone singing "Love Letters in the Sand," and the Lettermen with "Love Is a Many Splendored Thing." Those were the songs you listened to when you had your latest crush. Of course, songs like "Purple People Eater" and "Yakkity-Yak" were simply lots of fun. It is not surprising that the songs of the 50s are still the best remembered of the last century; and there wasn't a word of profanity or sexual innuendo in them. Concerts were something the high school band performed. And the raciest music event was Dick Clark's American Bandstand.

In those days there was no cable TV, and certainly no MTV. Al Gore had not yet invented the Internet. And video games would have to wait for another generation. As a boy I was busy building clubhouses in the nearby woods rather than playing the latest computer game. In my early teens my free time was spent riding horses and going camping. I didn't have to worry about things like AIDS, homosexuality, or sexually transmitted diseases. Those were the days when parents prided themselves on protecting their children and making sure they weren't growing up too fast. Kids were protected from "adult" conversations. Today, mothers put makeup on preschool children and dress preadolescents in provocative clothing, scared to death our daughters are going to be left behind. Little boys, who were once allowed to make up games and play ball during school recess, are forced into highly organized, incredibly competitive athletic programs before they're even in school. Many are never allowed to be little boys. It really is very sad!

The challenges of parenting in such an age as this are great. And making those challenges even greater are the powerful forces of modern media. Quite frankly, if you are going to minimize the negative impact of the media on your kids, you are going to have to swim upstream, go against the flow, and probably be charged with being a very old fashioned, mean parent. So be it! I want to start with some basic principles for dealing with the whole media issue. Then we'll look at some specifics having to do with certain types of media.

GET EDUCATED

Bob Waliszewski tells of meeting his wife and children for lunch at a restaurant. Seated nearby were a mother and her teenaged boys. One of the boys had on a T-shirt emblazoned with "KORN" in big letters across the front. When the boys took off, leaving the mother to pay the bill, Bob went over to her and asked, "Do you mind if I ask you a question?" She said she didn't, so he asked, "I was wondering how you handle the fact that one of your sons wears the T-shirt of a band whose lead singer fantasizes about brutally torturing his mother?" The mother got a look of horror on her face, gasped, and said, "I had no idea."[1]

That's the problem. Most parents have no idea what their children are watching or listening to. It amazes me how many otherwise intelligent parents allow their children to have cable TV or a computer hooked up to the Internet in their bedrooms. Even when their kids are in their presence, they're listening to music over headsets. So the parent is blissfully ignorant, even if their children are being fed the most vile, violent, rebellious, or provocative of content. Furthermore, kids are dropped at the movie to see a PG film, and it never enters the minds of their parents that kids regularly "movie hop," going from one theater to another, and may end up viewing the most violent or sexually explicit movie at the multiplex.

A couple of years ago, rapper Eminem surpassed all previous records for first-week sales by a solo artist for his recording project, *The Marshall Mathers LP*. Over 1.7 million copies were sold the first week, mostly to teens. Did you know that on the album the rapper boasts of raping his mother, snorting cocaine, and killing his wife? The album has since sold millions. Does that mean that millions of parents approved of these lyrics? No, it means that millions of parents don't care enough to know what they're kids are listening to.

Let me urge you to know what your kids are watching. Know what movies they actually see, not just the ones they claim to see. Listen to the music they are listening to. And check the browsers they use on the computer to see the sites they are visiting. Make it a point to know who the media stars are and what they stand for.

It takes time and a great investment of effort; but you need to get educated.

SET FAMILY STANDARDS

The late Fred Rogers of "Mr. Rogers Neighborhood" fame put his finger on a big problem in most homes. He said, "[Kids don't] really know if the family approves or disapproves of what is on [TV]. All they know is that the mother and father bought it, brought it in there and set it in the middle of the living room. And how are they to know that it really does or doesn't reflect the family tradition?"[2] While he spoke of TV, the same could be said for any and all types of media.

Thus it is important that family standards of what is acceptable and unacceptable need to be determined and communicated. A standard draws a line somewhere in the culture. But good standards are more than just prohibitive. Parents should discuss the reasons for the standard. Standard-setting should be viewed as a great opportunity for communication and for teaching our kids to be spiritually discerning. For younger children it is a parent's responsibility simply to say that this or that is acceptable or unacceptable. But as our kids grow older and more mature, we should not only discuss reasons for standards, but also seek and listen to their input as well.

We've always had a standard in our home that R-rated movies are unacceptable. We've had that standard as much to keep me from viewing movies that would not be good for me as to restrict our kids. There have been times when I've wanted to go see an R-rated movie that I felt had redeeming value but have stuck to that standard so as not to weaken my resolve not to see others that had no redeeming value. However, I think it was our son's senior year of high school that he came to me to confess that he and some friends had gone to see "Platoon." It was a highly acclaimed war movie, rated R for its graphic violence. It was one of those movies I would have wanted to see. I was disappointed in Shan for violating our family standard, but understood the basis on which he wanted to see the movie and was pleased that he was disappointed in himself for having disobeyed.

With the media, as with other areas of life, we parents need to choose our battles carefully. We should focus on what's really important and give our kids the freedom to make some mistakes in areas that aren't as important. Some parents' idea of setting standards is to outlaw everything: no movies, no television, no entertainment, period. Personally, I think that eventually it has a negative impact on the parent who doesn't know or care what their children are doing, where they're going, or what they are watching and listening to. One breeds rebellion; the other allows kids to feed on that which is terribly destructive. But setting reasonable standards is the proper balance. Now, if we could only agree on what is reasonable.

In their excellent book, *Reclaiming Your Family*,[3] Bob and Debra Bruce offer what they and their family use as a basis for determining television standards. However, you could modify these to apply to any form of media.

- Is the program something your child would choose to watch or is it just blaring noise?
- How much time has your child spent watching TV today? This week?
- If your child weren't watching TV, would he or she be engaged in a more productive activity such as exercise, reading, or interacting with friends?

- Does the show promote the Christian values that you believe in or that you are teaching your child?
- Does the program portray violence or graphic sexual activity? Does it focus negatively upon races? Does it treat all people equally or is one race or sex in control?
- Is the show something your child would choose to watch, or is it a habit at this time of day?
- Is there a program on public television at this time that might be educational for the child?
- Is your child old enough to understand that the program is make-believe or not real?
- Is the program uplifting, educational, or entertaining, or does it make you depressed and dull?
- Does the show promote your Christian family values?
- Are slang terms or offensive language used on the show something that might be picked up by your child?

The Bruces suggest you read these questions to your children and then select a television show that they enjoy and determine if it measures up.

EMPHASIZE BIBLICAL PRINCIPLES

The Bible says in Phil. 4:8, "Fix your thoughts on what is true and honorable and right. Think about things that are pure and lovely and admirable. Think about things that are excellent and worthy of praise."

The Bible says in Ps. 1:1-3, "Oh, the joys of those who do not follow the advice of the wicked, or stand around with sinners, or join in with scoffers. But they delight in doing everything the Lord wants; day and night they think about His law. They are like trees planted along the riverbank, bearing fruit each season without fail. Their leaves never wither, and in all they do, they prosper."

The Bible says in Ps. 101:3-5, "I will refuse to look at anything vile and vulgar. I hate all crooked dealings; I will have nothing to do with them. I will reject perverse ideas and stay away from every evil. I will not tolerate people who slander their neighbors. I will not endure conceit or pride."

It is not my intention here to do an exhaustive search of the scriptures concerning the biblical principles that should inform the control of media. But as we propose to raise "G-rated" kids in this "R-rated" world, nothing is more important than our worldview. Our worldview is developed, directed, and decided by our understanding of God's Word.

TELEVISION

Let's move from the world of generalities and principles to the specifics of controlling different types of media. Without a doubt, the greatest media influence in all of our lives in the western world is television. A study done several years ago by *TV Guide* reported that only 40 percent of Americans would give up TV even for a million dollars. That study by the Peter D. Hart Research Associates also discovered:

- 63 percent often watch while eating dinner, including 76 percent of those between eight and twenty-four.
- More than a third of viewers leave the set on for background noise.
- 29 percent fall asleep with the tube on.
- 42 percent turn on the TV when entering a room.[4]

In the interest of fairness it must be pointed out that there are many positives that can come from the use of any form of media, especially television. With the push of a button we can travel around the world, have the best seat in the arena to watch our favorite ball team, learn the latest political developments all over the globe, or be genuinely entertained in very wholesome ways.

The problem is that too often we let the negatives dominate. And the negatives are not just violence, explicit sexuality, profanity, and coarse humor. Television can teach our children to be unrealistic in thinking that most problems can be solved in thirty minutes, or really big ones in an hour. Television can give our kids a distorted view of reality, concerning what is good, beautiful, and important. Television tends to promote materialism by parading before our kids and us an endless array of products we have to have to be beautiful, successful, or fulfilled.

So the solution is not in banning television, but controlling it. How do you do that? First, you **set limits**. Choose to limit how many hours a day the television is on. On school nights television might be limited to one program. Some parents don't allow the TV on at all on school nights. But help your kids **choose shows** carefully. If they are limited in the number of shows they can watch, they will also be more discerning in choosing them.

Furthermore, they will discover other activities that may be far more satisfying. As you limit TV in your home, you'll have to be firm. Don't expect your kids to be pleased with such limitations, especially at the start. As a matter of fact, if the television has not been controlled in your home, your children will very likely go through actual withdrawal symptoms such as anger, temper tantrums, and moodiness.

Above all else, do not fall into the trap of using the television as a babysitter. It may be convenient, but your children pay the price. Excessive television viewing has a direct and negative relation to obesity, violence, aggressive behavior, and negative values related to drugs, alcohol, promiscuity, and racial stereotypes. Surely you don't want that sort of a babysitter.

We've talked a lot in previous chapters about looking for teachable moments. Watching TV together gives you the opportunity to **discuss with your kids what they've seen**. This is especially valuable when in the midst of an otherwise good show something is presented that violates your standards or contradicts your beliefs. The next commercial is a great time to hit the mute button and discuss with your children what they've just seen. And speaking of commercials, they too provide great opportunities to discuss family values. What really constitutes success? Do we really need to drive a certain kind of car to feel good about ourselves? Why do people want or need alcohol to make them happy? How important is outward beauty?

But the bottom line in controlling the television is to **turn it off**. If the program is offensive, turn it off. If there's nothing on that you *really* want to watch, turn it off. If the television is a distraction, keeping your kids or you from doing something that needs to get done, turn it off. If no one is watching it, turn it off. And sometimes, just to prove to yourself that you can do it—turn it off.

Let me close this section with a word about specialized TV offerings. We have had basic cable at our house for many years. Sports and news, the primary objects of my viewing tastes, are enhanced by basic cable as are my wife's favorites, old movies and early television sitcoms such as Lucy, Andy, and Beaver. We have never allowed the premium cable channels such as HBO, Showtime, or Cinemax into our home. I'm sure there must be some decent programming, but that decency is more than offset by the pipeline of filth each one provides. And while my children did not need that temptation, neither did I nor do I. Mom or Dad, you wouldn't put a bowl of poisoned food on your dinner table. So why put spiritual and moral poison in front of your children via the TV.

MTV is standard with most basic channel packages. But I can assure you that it was also forbidden in our home. Can anyone tell me anything good that has come from MTV? I believe it has been one of the most negative factors in modern-day teen culture. I'm writing soon after the 2004 Super Bowl Halftime fiasco produced by MTV. Raunchy, filthy, immodest, profane, sexually explicit, and anti-patriotic are just some of the words that have been used to describe that show. But why should that be surprising when MTV is itself all of that.

Satellite television takes TV programming, good and bad, into previously unreached areas of the world. I saw a special on the nation of Bhutan, the Himalayan Mountain Kingdom, which has basically been isolated from the world. Their king was being interviewed about his attempts to keep what he considered to be western decadence out of his kingdom but admitted to fighting a losing battle as satellite dishes were now conspicuous all over the country. Again, that could be good. Satellite technology is taking the Christian gospel to places it could not otherwise go. Countries ruled by despots can no longer keep their people in ignorance of the freedom of hundreds of millions of people living outside their countries. But that same technology brings more and more negative influences into all the homes receiving it as well.

WHAT ABOUT MOVIES?

The same standards that were listed for choosing television programming are appropriate for guiding movie selection. We still have our "no R-rated movie" policy, although it is our servant rather than our master. Jan and I both saw the R-rated *The Passion of the Christ* and urged every adult and older teen to see it. However, the reason for the rating was obvious, the incredible brutality Christ experienced. That brutality was real and needs to be understood by us all. Upon returning from a vacation in Scotland we rented and watched *Braveheart*, eager to better understand the story of the Scottish hero, Henry Wallace. But the "no R-rated" policy remains self-imposed, except in the most extreme exceptions even though our children are grown and gone.

Actually, the movie rating policy Hollywood has imposed upon itself is far from perfect. Aside from the fact that we should all avoid NC-17 films, and I believe we should avoid R-rated films, the fact is that many PG-13 films should be rated R and many PG films should be rated PG-13. Parents should read the reviews and do their homework before attending any movie, let alone taking their kids. Approving the movies your kids attend without your being with them is an even greater responsibility.

WHAT ABOUT MUSIC?

You can't control what your kids listen to when they're not with you. But you can communicate family standards that you expect them to conform to. We made it a practice in our home to listen to every cassette or CD our kids brought home. If they bought it, even with their own money, if it was objectionable it went into the trash. That causes kids to think twice before acquiring a new album. Quite honestly, there were supposedly Christian albums that didn't make the cut.

I know of Christian parents who try to limit their teens to only Christian music. First, let me remind you that there really is no such thing as Christian music, only Christian lyrics. And there is certainly secular music that is not objectionable. My son was really into U-2, Phil Collins, and Genesis and I probably listened to every project they completed while my son was at home. We went to U-2 and Genesis concerts together with his friends and had a blast. I also went with both my kids to Christian concerts by artists like Petra, DeGarmo & Key, and others who would not have been my personal choice. But those were great bonding times, and I must admit that those artists had a great Christian witness.

EVERYTHING ELSE

We've not dealt at all with video games, although many of the same principles apply. The same is true in regard to the explosion of radio choices, digital recording, and copying. There is the dramatic increase of all types of electronic games, text messaging, cellular phones, personal pagers, and a host of yet-to-be-invented products that are going to more and more invade the privacy of the home and challenge the values of parents. Parenting is not for the fainthearted. It is a greater challenge than ever before.

Nowhere is that challenge greater than in all the issues surrounding personal computers. Let me go on record as saying as strongly as possible that no teen or preteen has any business with a computer in his or her room unless it has no possible connection to the Internet and is used exclusively for schoolwork. It is simply too great a temptation. Even if nothing of an offensive nature is accessed, huge amounts of time can be wasted if there is no accountability. But the availability of not only pornographic sites but chat rooms where predators prey on unsuspecting teens makes it way outside the bounds of reason for a parent to give such access to their kids.

IN CONCLUSION

Obviously, the subject of controlling the media is a huge one with so many different tentacles that it is very difficult to contain. However, there are some overriding principles that come to bear regardless of the media arena in which we're involved.

First, there is the *discernment* principle. It is obvious that not all media messages are good for you or your children. But where do you draw the line? Based on a biblically informed, Christian worldview, there will be many black and white issues where the placement of that line will be obvious. But there will also be gray areas where the placement of that line is not nearly so obvious and may vary from child to child and circumstance to circumstance. No one, not even this author, although most things are pretty black and white for me, can set all the standards or put in place all the guidelines by which your family should operate. But you can pray for spiritual discernment.

Second, there is the *moderation* principle. Some parents simply forbid access to media of all sorts. It seems to me that such an approach always produces resentment and most likely encourages the child to be devious and deceitful. However, "anything goes" is a recipe for spiritual, moral, relational, and familial disaster. A healthy situation is one in which families enjoy the benefits of the media while upholding standards that protect from most of the liabilities, all the while developing growing maturity on the part of their children.

Finally, there is the principle of *integration*. Television programs, movies, music (Christian and secular), things learned from the Internet, and things both good and bad gathered from all sorts of media sources need to be integrated into family discussions and used both as illustrative and motivational for the development and maintaining of family standards. But when all else is said and done, don't be afraid to say no.

No one can deny that media has a profound impact on culture. Indeed, many times the line between media and reality become blurred. Three years ago we had planned to take our kids and their spouses on a family vacation to Ireland. However, in the midst of all those plans, Shan and Lise got pregnant. We ended up taking a trip with Jennifer and Darren to Russia, but told Shan and Lise that when they were ready we would still take them to Ireland. When our grandson, Jack, was a year old we had that window of opportunity because they already knew they wanted to get pregnant again. So we planned our trip for that summer with Jack staying with Aunt Jennifer and Uncle Darren.

Shan and Lise are great parents and, among other things, they videotaped Jack's favorite stories and songs so they could be played in their absence. I think that deep down inside they were also thinking that if something were to happen and they were not to return that Jack would have something to remember them by. Upon our arrival in Ireland, Shan and Lise called home and were told that Jack was doing great and that Jennifer had shown him the video. She said he had called out, "Da-da-da-da, Ma-ma-ma-ma!" But what she waited to tell all of us until we safely returned home was this. When she showed Jack the video he did say, "Da-da-da-da, Ma-ma-ma-ma," But he also ran across the room as fast as his little legs would carry him, spread his arms out so as to try to embrace the TV and sobbed and sobbed as though his heart would break.

It is very easy to see what is represented by the media as the real thing. Let's make sure that what our kids see and hear in that regard is worthy of being embraced.

Chapter Nine

Deal with Substance Abuse

Almost every edition of the local paper brings news of yet another tragic death of a teen who consumed alcohol, drove a car, and ended up in the morgue. For each fatality, who knows how many other teens barely dodged the bullet? I recently read that one out of five high school seniors admits to being drunk at least once a week. Actually, alcohol far outdistances marijuana as the drug of choice among American teens. That is not to say that pot, and other even harder drugs, are not a problem, for we all know they are. Let's face it, we live in a society where alcohol and drugs are readily accessible and where society as a whole hardly lifts an eyebrow to drinking and so-called recreational drugs.

The fact is that substance abuse of any kind destroys self-discipline. It often leads to disinterest in anything challenging or worthwhile. Schoolwork suffers, personal appearance is often neglected, family relationships are stressed, and friendships are often abandoned. Furthermore, as Christians, we know that drunkenness is a sin (Rom. 13:13, Gal. 5:21, Eph. 5:18, 1 Pet. 4:3, 1 Cor. 6:10, Luke 21:34, etc.). The Bible also gives practical warnings against intoxication (Prov. 20:1; 23:29-35, etc.). By observation and experience we know the dangers of alcohol and drug use. So how do we keep our kids from falling into the trap of substance abuse? Or if they have already gotten involved, how do we help them get out of that trap?

I wish I could write from a background of having avoided this trap myself. But the truth is that, although I was raised in a non-drinking, Christian home, and although I professed to be a Christian, social drinking was very much a part of my later high school and early college days, and getting drunk wasn't uncommon to me. I'm ashamed of the fact that I succumbed to peer pressure in that area of my life. And while drugs were not a part of my life, that's probably more because of a lack of availability than of any moral resistance. Yes, I knew this was wrong. I knew many of the dangers. I knew it would greatly disappoint my parents. I knew it was illegal. And by most standards, I was a pretty decent kid. So if I went down that road in the early sixties, what is to hold a kid back today when both availability and acceptance have increased dramatically?

I'm pleased to tell you that both of my kids avoided this temptation. My daughter, Jennifer, is a crusader of near Carry Nation convictions on the subject. And among my treasured letters is one from my son, Shan, when he was a freshman in college. He had attended a Christian event where he had been very disappointed in the behavior of some of the teens from our church. Jan and I were asleep when he came home that night. But when he got home he wrote a note and left it on our dresser for me to find the next morning. With his permission, here's what he wrote:

> "Dad, Good Morning! I hope you had a good time last night. The program was excellent. But afterwards was weird. I felt different, like I was holding the other kids back or something. I was brought up different than them. I have standards. I know that sounds cocky, but it's true. I'll tell you the truth. I have never done anything immoral, I have never used illegal drugs, I have never smoked, and I have never had a drink. Nothing! I'm proud of that, but I just have trouble relating sometimes. Have a great day. I really love you lots. Thanks for all you've done. Love, Shan"

As I've said again and again, Jan and I don't claim to be perfect parents, but looking back, I realize that we could have done a whole lot more to guard our kids from the temptations of substance abuse. We did some things right. Furthermore, I've learned more than I ever wanted to know through experience as a pastor. So let me share with you five "E" verbs that can help you deal with all the issues relating to your kids and substance abuse.

EXAMINE

Parents should first of all examine their own lifestyle to determine what sort of example they are setting for their kids. Children learn that drinking and drugs are acceptable first of all by observing their parents. If drinking is part of your social practice, you will find it difficult to convince your kids that there are real dangers associated with it. If you pop a pill to relax, why should your kids believe that drugs are something to be avoided? My father and mother were teetotalers, and while I didn't live up to their example, I *knew* I was wrong.

Children also develop convictions about drugs and alcohol from an early age by how their parents react to depictions of substance abuse. Is drunkenness in a sitcom viewed as hilarious, or do you use it as a teaching moment? What about commercials for alcohol on television? Unfortunately, the beer commercials are probably the catchiest and most entertaining on TV. Many preschoolers have been heard singing a beer jingle, not even knowing what they're singing about. You probably can't totally shield your impressionable young children from such influences, but you can turn them around and use them as opportunities early on to develop moral and biblical convictions in your children.

I'll never forget the night in Oregon when the local pastor took my family and me to a local Shakey's Pizza Parlor to eat following the services. We were in the midst of consuming our pizza and pop when the waitress brought a pitcher of beer to a neighboring table. As the men at the table poured the frothy liquid into chilled glasses, our three-year-old son stood up on his chair, pointed his finger, and said in a voice loud enough to be heard by everyone present, "Look, Dad, those bad men are drinking beer!" I don't even remember having had a discussion on the subject, but obviously the convictions reflected in the letter I quoted earlier began to develop very early on.

Examine what you are teaching your children by your personal example and by your attitude toward the practices of others. By the way, everyone in the pizza parlor laughed, including the men who went on drinking their beer. And it was another teaching moment as I explained to Shan that while drinking was not a good thing, the fact that those men were drinking did not in itself make them bad men either. Indeed, God loved them very much.

EXPOSE

Suppose you have a teenager or even younger child and you suspect they are drinking or doing drugs. What should you do? Most importantly, you should not deny your suspicions. Physiologically, the younger the abuser the faster the rate of addiction, so it is critical that you intercede as soon as possible if such abuse is going on. And while drinking may be obvious by behavior we all recognize to be consistent with intoxication or even by smell, use of pot, speed, or even harder drugs may not be as easy to discern.

However, Dr. James Dobson, in his book, *The New Dare to Discipline*, lists eight physical and emotional symptoms of drug abuse:[1]

1. Inflammation of the eyelids and nose is common. The pupils of the eyes are either very wide or very small, depending on the kind of drugs used.

2. Extremes of energy may be represented. The individual may be sluggish, gloomy, and withdrawn or loud, hysterical, and jumpy.

3. The appetite is extreme, either very great or very poor. Weight loss may occur.

4. The personality suddenly changes. The individual may become irritable, inattentive and confused, or aggressive, suspicious, and explosive.

5. Body and breath odor is often bad. Cleanliness may be ignored.

6. The digestive system may be upset; diarrhea, nausea, and vomiting may occur. Headaches and double vision are also common. Other signs of physical deterioration may include change in skin tone and body stance.

7. With intravenous drug users, needle marks on the body, usually appearing on the arms, are an important symptom. These punctures sometimes get infected and appear as sores and boils.

8. Moral values often crumble and are replaced by new, outlandish ideas and values.

The fact is, different drugs produce different symptoms. Furthermore, some of these symptoms could be produced by something having nothing to do with drugs. But if any of these symptoms or some other red flag raises your suspicions, don't deny them. Denial may be the most difficult barrier to a parent helping his or her child. I've seen it again and again.

We've always had a very active youth program, and it has never been uncommon for kids from other churches to attend many functions at Kingsway. The son of an associate pastor at an area church had gotten involved in our youth program and often attended our Sunday night service. I saw this young man come into one such service with a friend from our congregation. I prayed just before the sermon and when I looked up, I noticed that they were both gone. A few minutes into my sermon I saw one of our youth coaches come back into the auditorium and call another youth coach outside. Later I learned that the young man had gotten violently ill. The youth coaches actually took him home and put him to bed. In the midst of all that he readily admitted that he had smoked some bad pot on an empty stomach that had made him so sick he had nearly vomited his guts out, and he had almost passed out as well.

I prayed and counseled with other staff about what to do. But I knew if this boy had been my son I would have wanted to know about it, as the dad had been at his own church when the incident happened. So I called him and asked him if we could talk. He chose to come to my office. When I told him of what had happened he became enraged, not toward his son, but toward me. He ranted and raved about my defaming his son and how he ought to bring legal action against the church for suggesting his son would do such a thing. His face was red as a beet, he doubled his fist up in front of my face and told me he ought to come across that desk and clean my clock or words to that effect. I need to tell you that his son had some tough days ahead, because his dad was in total denial of the truth.

Several kids had told both our youth pastor and myself about one of our kids who was not only using, but was dealing drugs at a local high school. Our youth pastor confronted the teen, who angrily denied it. But the evidence was overwhelming. So our youth pastor went to talk to the parents who were as adamant as the pastor dad I just told you about that their son would never do such a thing. They threw the youth pastor out of the house and told him never to come back. Surprisingly, they continued to attend our church. The boy was never arrested. He went off to college, and, while there, found a personal relationship with the Lord. He came forward one Sunday at Kingsway to apologize to the church as well as to Larry and me for his drug using and dealing days, as well as for the pain he had caused us. However, never a word of apology was received from the parents.

So don't go into denial. Force your way through any deception and secrecy that may be surrounding your child's life. Talk with his or her friends' parents, his or her teachers, even your neighbors if you suspect such abuse. Put your child's welfare above any personal embarrassment. Don't think for a moment that it couldn't happen to your kid. While laws restricting the availability of alcohol are now more rigidly enforced, all it takes is someone of age, who is willing to buy for their friends. And how many stories have we heard, or even personal situations have we encountered, where parents actually buy the booze for the kids. As for drugs, I doubt there's a teenager in your church who couldn't tell who is dealing and where.

EXPLAIN

We've stressed the importance of parent-child communication throughout the pages of this book. Nowhere is that more important than in combating substance abuse. Advertising for alcohol is remarkably entertaining. Television and movies glorify both alcohol and drugs as fun and perfectly acceptable. Your task as a parent is to give the other side of the story.

A Christian parent should certainly discuss with their kids such scriptures as those mentioned earlier in this chapter. There should be no doubt as to what the biblical standard is. In addition to scriptures on drunkenness, your kids should know what the Bible says about how we should treat our bodies (1 Cor. 6:19-20), who should control our lives (Eph. 5:18-20), and the example we should set for others (1 Cor. 10:23-11:1). While communicating should not turn to nagging, every story about teens killed while driving drunk, about kids whose minds have been destroyed by drugs, about kids being arrested and suffering the consequences, should be woven into family conversations on a regular basis.

There is a young man lying in a vegetative state in a nursing facility not far from our church. Several members of his family are also members of our church family. He, in what his parents believe was a one-time fling, overdosed on heroine. Regardless of the circumstances, the results are the same, a healthy teenager was left with his mind destroyed. It is a powerful, painful reminder of the dangers of substance abuse. I wish every parent could take their kids to visit him. His example would speak to them more eloquently than the most polished of words. And the way his parents' world has been turned upside down, would impress upon every parent how important it is that we intercede at the first sign of any form of substance abuse.

ENGAGE

I know it is only another stanza of the same song, but I cannot overemphasize how important it is that parents work at engaging their children in close personal relationships. Not only will the child be less susceptible to outside, negative peer pressure, and not only is the parent better able to explain the dangers of substance abuse and the positives of a totally sober life, the parent is also in a position to better see the telltale signs if such abuse ever begins.

As my children were growing up there were many conversations about their friends and acquaintances who were getting into things they shouldn't have been getting into. I respected the confidentiality of my children every bit as much as I would that of a pastor-parishioner counseling session. However, I was often able to help them help their friends. Furthermore, they knew they could come to me to discuss any and all personal problems. And on the occasions they came to me to discuss their own behavior that had not been up to our family standards, they knew there wouldn't be a blow-up, which would have served only to alienate and polarize. Instead they knew there would be a reasoned discussion, and, if there were consequences, they would also be reasoned, as opposed to overreaction, at least most of the time.

EVADE

Much of what we've said thus far has focused on reacting to suspicions of drug abuse. While several of the principles we've discussed certainly contribute to prevention as well, it is important to do everything we can to insure that our kids never start down the road to substance abuse. I believe that starts with an understanding of why alcohol and drugs are so attractive to kids in the first place. In an article by Ted Stone and Philip Barber, they list ten specific reasons:

1. **Curiosity:** We are all intrigued by the unknown. Investigation is a part of growing up. This curiosity if further encouraged by all the positive descriptions in media advertisements or by the recommendations of those already drinking or using.

2. **The desire to feel good:** Drugs and alcohol have become escape mechanisms for many. People often brag of the relaxing feeling delivered by their drug of choice. Tranquilizers provide a false, peaceful serenity.

3. **Negative peer pressure:** Hey, I didn't even like the taste of alcohol. It was for me—and probably most kids—at the start, a way of fitting in.

4. **Poor self-concept:** Those who focus on their shortcomings often find a temporary measure of comfort in mind-altering substances.

5. **The desire to be cool:** Closely identified with peer pressure, there is an image promoted by the media that links concepts of success and happiness to alcohol and drugs.

6. **To cope with difficult problems:** Physical and emotional difficulties often drive people to find assistance in the artificial world of drugs.

7. **Rebellion:** Although rules and laws are necessary for the benefit of all mankind, many people reject the burden of responsibility. Tragically, many who seek freedom from moral order find instead a horrible slavery to a cruel master.

8. **Lack of a Christian worldview:** Although not all professing Christians practice the principle, Christianity certainly teaches the importance of a clear mind and clean body. Christ gives meaning and direction to life that the lost person does not have.

9. **The poor example of family and/or friends:** That's where we began, and the importance of a good example cannot be overstated. You would think that the child of an alcoholic would hate alcohol and that the child of an addict would hate drugs, But instead, the example often pulls the next generation in as well.

10. **Other reasons:** There are many, such as the delusion of invincibility, the accessibility of drugs, an escape from boredom, and relief from pain.

So the first tool in evading substance abuse in the lives of your kids is to understand why such abuse is desirable in the first place.

Closely related to understanding is education. Our kids are always being exposed to information about drugs and alcohol from various forms of media. However, not all of it is accurate, and it is most often slanted toward the agenda of the presenter. Such is certainly the case with the "Drink Responsibly" campaigns of the alcohol companies. That's like putting the fox in charge of protecting the chicken house. But truth is a wonderful prevention tool, and education begins at home. Our kids should be encouraged to seek the truth about any issues that concern them. But it is our responsibility as parents to make sure they are getting good information. It is in part the responsibility of the church to make sure that good educational resources are made available.

One of the most important ways to evade the problems of substance abuse is by helping our children develop positive peer pressure. Peer pressure works both ways; and as surely as getting in with the wrong crowd may lead to substance abuse, getting in with the right crowd helps to guard against it. Most of our children's close friends were from good Christian homes, and we knew their parents. That gave us an advantage. But Shan had a group of five or six buddies in junior high and high school, not all of whom were Christians, but all were committed to high moral standards. They considered kids who drank, smoked, did drugs, and slept around to be weak and not worthy of their company. They were a popular group of guys who were well known for their stance, and that served them and us well.

Some of you may remember Nancy Reagan's "Just Say No" campaign. Liberals and sophisticates loved to make fun of what they considered an unworkable, simplistic approach to evading substance abuse. But the fact is that we should teach our kids how to say no. Gertrude Atherton wrote a novel, *Ruler of Kings*, in which a rich man sent his son to be raised in a poor home. The person raising him required the boy to say no 20 times the first thing in the morning and the last thing at night. Plutarch said that the people of Asia became vassals largely because they could not say no.

Closely akin to teaching our kids to say no is providing them with preplanned responses. Sometimes negative peer pressure makes it very difficult for our kids to say no, but they are strong enough to use a face-saving response when asked to smoke or drink something they know to be wrong. "Sorry, I'm allergic to smoke." "Alcohol and I don't get along." "Not today. I'm just not in the mood."

"My parents always smell my breath and they would ground me for the rest of my life." "I'm really into health and fitness and this doesn't fit into my lifestyle." Sure, just saying, "No," is even better; but sometimes our kids need a crutch.

Getting your kids involved in worthwhile activities is also a plus in evading substance abuse. Boredom is often a precursor to drug and alcohol experimentation. If a teen is finding satisfaction in exciting, meaningful activities that reward and enrich, the perceived need for drugs or alcohol is greatly diminished.

Let me again point out that it is important that your teens learn from the tragic mistakes of others. The death of a star athlete resulting from driving drunk; the brain damage of a popular girl due to her experimentation with drugs; the honor student who lost his scholarship to an Ivy League school because of his drug conviction; the kid who was active in church who is now behind bars because he did something stupid while on drugs. All these real life dramas make the newspapers again and again as well as the informal newsgathering processes of your child. Such real life stories should be the fodder for ongoing discussions between parents and their children.

However, for Christian kids, the greatest tool in evading substance abuse is a close personal relationship with the Lord. True success in all the important arenas of life comes from real dependence on the God of the universe to inspire and guide us and give us the strength to avoid the life-traps that the evil one is always setting for us. As parents we should do everything possible to encourage spiritual growth in our children and to provide them with the best possible support system for continued spiritual growth.

Of course, all this presupposes a positive example by you. That's where we began, by urging you to examine your lifestyle. Teaching your kids to do as you say and not as you do is a waste of time and energy for both of you. But a well-lived, godly life of abstinence from alcohol and drugs will go a long way in positively impacting your children.

IN CONCLUSION

It is a heavy responsibility to be a parent. Lots of moms and dads want to be their child's buddy instead of assuming the responsibilities of parenthood. Listen, you've got to ask the tough questions. Your child's welfare is at stake. Here are some of the most basic:

- Where are you going to be (with phone number and address)?
- How are you going to get there?
- With whom are you going?
- Who else will be there?
- Will adults be present? Who?
- What time will you be leaving?
- What time will you be home?
- What will you do if drugs or alcohol are present? Leave immediately or call us and we'll come get you.

If your teens aren't responsible enough to answer such questions, they aren't responsible enough to be out on their own. A few weekends of watching old westerns with Mom and Dad should encourage responsibility. Sure your kids will see such questions and the rules that accompany them as limiting. But if you have that communication thing going that I keep talking about they'll also know all this is for their protection and because you love them.

What if you discover that your kids really are involved in substance abuse? What if it's too late to evade? What if you examine, expose, explain, and engage, and yet you really haven't gotten anywhere? Then it's time to get professional help; the sooner the better. For substance abuse doesn't only destroy relationships, it destroys lives.

Chapter Ten

Lead Them to Christ

Both of my children accepted Jesus as Savior and were baptized at an early age. That is not surprising, seeing that they were both exposed to the gospel basically from the day they were born. As a matter of fact, Shan was born while Jan and I were traveling in full-time evangelistic work. Thus, he was in church six nights a week, heard his dad preach about Jesus again and again, and saw people responding to the gospel on a daily basis.

When Shan was three we were in an evangelistic crusade in Ohio. I can see it as if it were yesterday. Most often he found other kids to play with after church. But this night he waited patiently for me as I greeted people at the door following the service. Then he came up to me, and in complete seriousness he asked, "Daddy, will you baptize me?" I maintained my composure sufficiently to ask, "Why do you want to be baptized, son?" To which he answered, "So I can eat crackers and drink grape juice too." He associated baptism with the ability to take the Lord's Supper, and rightly so. He was putting things together, and that's good, but it was obvious that as a three year old he did not possess the understanding or the need to accept Jesus as his Savior.

Both Shan and Jennifer were baptized into Christ near their seventh birthday, Shan just after and Jennifer just before. Frankly, we had previously discouraged them, questioning their understanding until through persistence and the way they answered our questions, we were convinced they were genuine in their understanding and their profession of faith.

Actually, I was raised in a Christian home where I was taken to church from my first Sunday on earth. Therefore, it is not surprising that I came to faith in Christ at the early age of nine. Oh, I had always believed in Jesus from the time I believed anything. I had always loved Jesus. My parents loved Jesus, and they taught me to do so too. However, it occurred to me as a nine-year-old that I was a sinner. No, I'd never murdered anyone or even stolen so much as a candy bar. But I had disobeyed my parents. I had lied. I had done any number of things that I knew to be wrong, that I knew to be disappointing to God. I also knew that for my sins to be forgiven someone had to take the punishment. And I knew that Jesus, God's Son had already done so on the cross. Furthermore, I knew that if I accepted Jesus as my Savior, He would forgive my sins, come into my life, and save me. I talked to my mom and dad about life's most important decision, and I talked to our preacher as well. But on a June Sunday in 1953, when the invitation was extended to come to Christ, I walked forward at the Loyal Christian Church in Springfield, Missouri, and gave my life to Jesus. Our tiny church didn't have a baptistry. But that afternoon our church family gathered on the banks of the James River south of Springfield where I was baptized into Christ. Though I have not always been faithful, there is no doubt in my mind that I knew what I was doing and that my conversion was real.

Both my children and I came to Christ at a very early age and very naturally so because of the homes in which we were raised. Jan was not raised in a Christian home, though one-by-one her family came to Christ. But even so she accepted Christ as her Lord and Savior at the age of twelve, largely because of a neighbor who faithfully took her and her sisters to church.

There are many parents who understand their children's need for love, attention, food, clothing, shelter, education, and a hundred other things that are necessary or to be desired. And yet those same parents may ignore the most important ingredient in anyone's life, a personal faith in the Lord, the only contribution we can make to the lives of our children that has eternal consequences. Therefore, many of today's children lack a sense of purpose in their lives, the morality that is attached to faith, and the assurance of everlasting life through Jesus Christ. And while the world refuses to acknowledge it, that fact accounts for much of the turmoil we find in our society today, especially among young people.

THE SIGNIFICANCE OF FAITH

A personal relationship with God through faith in Christ gives true meaning to life. It explains where we came from, why we're here, and where we're going. Such faith allows us to face each new day with the confidence that God loves us, cares for us, and is with us. Such faith defines how we relate to others, our sense of priorities, our morality, and most importantly how we relate to God Himself.

However, it is important to realize that such faith does not just happen. The development of faith is a lifelong process, but it is best and most easily facilitated in the home. Just as a baby must learn to crawl before he can walk and walk before he can run, so faith develops sequentially. In his book, *Will Our Children Have Faith*, author John Westerhoff III tells us there are four stages in the development of faith:[1]

1. **Experienced faith:** A small child believes only what he has experienced. He thinks in concrete terms, and the abstract is incomprehensible. This faith is determined by what the child observes in other people. Westerhoff says that this stage is highlighted by action and reaction toward others and events.

2. **Affiliate faith:** The child, teen, or adult's faith is formed by affiliating with significant people and events. For the person raised in a Christian home, the church and its activities take on special significance. Belonging to a group and feeling a part of something important is very significant.

3. **Searching faith:** There comes a time in which a person begins to use his or her mind to ask critical questions and to make

important judgments. During this stage of faith, development is not unusual for a person to take a serious look at other belief systems and alternative courses of action.

4. **Owned faith:** This is the ultimate—when faith becomes personal. It is no longer dependent upon Mom and Dad, upon mentors, or upon what anyone else thinks. You know what you believe and are passionate about it.

I can identify with all four stages. Growing up in a Christian home, I had an experiential faith based on what I saw in the lives of my parents and what they taught me. I mentioned that I accepted Christ when I was nine years old. My faith was genuine, but it was basically one I had inherited from my parents, and it became an affiliate faith as I became a part of the church. There came a time when my faith was basically put on hold. However, as a pre-med major at a state university, I had my inherited faith challenged by unbelieving professors. And while I was not living out even my inherited faith, their challenge did move to me to start searching for answers. That was a time of searching faith. The result was that in the spring semester of my sophomore year I sincerely and wholeheartedly rededicated my life to Christ with a faith that was tested, found valid, and now was my very own.

Christian parents should consider it both a privilege and responsibility to help their kids progress through those stages of faith, and hopefully to complete the process more quickly than I did. Certainly, all those things that lead to faith building in our children should be a priority in our homes.

THE ROLE OF THE CHURCH

While our emphasis in this book is on the role of the parent, part of that role is involving others in the raising of our kids and the development of their faith. Nothing is more important in that regard than their involvement in a Bible-believing, Christ-honoring church. And in answer to one of the most often asked as well as most lame questions, "Should I make my children go to church?" the answer is yes. "But what if they don't want to go?" Do they always want to go to school? No. Do you make them go anyway? Do they want to go to the dentist? Never! Do you make them go anyway? A parent is charged with requiring what is best for their children, not necessarily that which is desired by their children. Now it is obviously better if a child wants to go to school and wants to go to church.

I believe that the church has a responsibility as much as possible without compromising to make its activities attractive and enjoyable. However, the often-voiced, adult excuse, "I was made to go to church when I was a kid so I don't want to go now," has no more validity than, "My parents made me take baths, so now that I'm an adult I'll never bathe again." Or "Mom and Dad made me do chores around the house so now that I'm an adult I'm not doing anything around the house."

Having said that children should be required to go to church, I must also caution that such a requirement will be seen only as hypocritical unless the parents are faithful in worship as well. To send your kids to church while you sleep in or go fishing teaches them something all right, but it's not what you want them to learn. Commitment as a family to a specific body of believers, and faithfulness to that body is an important teaching tool in the development of your children's faith.

Please believe me when I say that the lessons learned begin from the earliest age. That baby held in the arms of a dedicated church nursery worker lays a foundation for faith supported by the love and acceptance experienced in the context of a family of faith. And as the children progress from nursery to toddler to preschool to elementary age, each teacher, helper, and youth coach along the way makes a contribution to your child's faith.

Although my children have long since left the nest, they still recall the impact that people like Bill Branson and Jeff and Cheryl Harris made on their lives.

I can remember a new Christian working with preschoolers— including my own little pig-tailed girl, Jennifer. And of how Lynn read the Bible story only to have Jennifer shake her head and say, "That's not how my daddy pronounces that name," or correct her on some detail of the story. But studying the Scriptures with a caring teacher in Bible School or graded worship or "Little Lambs," greatly contributed to the spiritual growth of my kids. It wasn't just the teaching, it was even more the modeling of the Christian life by older kids and by adults my kids respected and loved.

Kingsway, the church in which my children grew up, has always been a healthy, growing church. Thus my children's experiences relating to the church were with very few exceptions healthy and positive. In their teen years the conferences, rallies, and conventions they attended, the choirs and activities such as Bible Bowl in which they participated, and the influence of the youth pastors on their lives, have all had a cumulative impact in the development of their faith. Christian friendships were developed that are still intact and most likely will be for a lifetime, in spite of the fact that their youth groups have long since been dispersed to many distant destinations.

Let me add one more incredibly important aspect of your child's involvement in the church. It is the only place, outside of the home, where absolute truth to guide your child's life is being taught. Mel and Norma Gabler in their book, *What Are They Teaching Our Children?* remind us:

> The only absolute truth in modern humanistic education is that there are no absolute values. All values must be questioned, especially home or church acquired values. Discard the experience gained from thousands of years of Western civilization. Instead, treat the students as primitive savages in the area of values. Let them select their own from slanted, inadequate information. Nothing, absolutely nothing, is certain. There are no universal rules, absolutely none.[2]

So parents, you need the church. You desperately need the church, first for yourselves, for you cannot be the spiritual mentors for your children that you need to be unless you are strong spiritually yourselves. However, you also need the church to reinforce the values and absolute truths that are so vital to your children's well being.

THE ROLE OF THE FAMILY

If you as a Christian adult took on the responsibility for mentoring three or four younger Christians, you would automatically recognize that three or four things are essential to the success of your efforts. You would have to dedicate some quality time, even sacrificial time to getting to know them. You would want to discover what their needs were. You would want to be open and transparent with them, even letting them know your faults and inadequacies. And, of course, you would want to share God's Word with those you were mentoring, helping them to be able to discern truth from error.

Whether you realized it or not, when those kids of yours were conceived, you were taking on the role of mentoring them, shaping those little lives into what God would have them become. And those issues of time, discovery of needs, transparency, and teaching God's Word are even more important in your role as the primary mentors to your kids. When you take them to church and make it a priority, when you pray before meals, when you read the Bible or Bible stories to them and pray with them at bedtime, that is all a part of spiritual mentoring.

Actually, the model for spiritual mentoring in the home is a passage we looked at earlier, Deut. 11:18-21:

> So commit yourselves completely to these words of mine. Tie them to your hands as a reminder, and wear them on your forehead. Teach them to your children. Talk about them when you are at home and when you are away on a journey; when you are lying down and when you are getting up again. Write them on the doorposts of your house and on your gate, so that as long as the sky remains above the earth, you and your children may flourish in the land the Lord swore to give your ancestors.

So how are those verses lived out in the context of New Testament Christianity? The text suggests that children need to be brought to a living faith in God through the normal experiences of everyday life. What sort of experiences are we talking about?

CULTIVATING FAITH

First, a parent needs to have a personal relationship with Christ as Lord and Savior. Then that parent needs to be living out their faith on a day-by-day basis. Kids can easily identify phoniness and hypocrisy.

Do you put into practice such principles as honesty, sacrificial love, and compassion on a daily basis?

Looking back with the perspective of many years, I realize that my parents modeled faith in Christ in ways that I did not recognize at the time. My father was in business and was successful, but he was also honest. Everyone respected my dad for his honesty. He defied the often-repeated axiom that you can't be successful in business and be honest. Yet my dad was, and I knew it was because he was a Christian.

I had one sister, and Dorothy was handicapped, having suffered brain damage at birth. Both her physical handicaps and her behavioral problems made her very difficult to care for, yet my mother sacrificially cared for her until Dorothy's death at more than 50 years of age. When I was a young boy, my Grandmother Larimore suffered a terrible stroke that left her bedfast and totally helpless for seven years. Yet my mother cared for her in our home, without complaint. Most often my mother could be heard singing hymns around the house, for it was her faith in Christ that both motivated and sustained her in caring for my sister and grandmother.

Both my parents loved and served the Lord, but it was my mother who had the greatest influence on me spiritually, simply by virtue of the time she spent with me. She talked to me about the Lord. She taught me to pray. She taught me to memorize scripture long before I was old enough to read. Let me urge you to do the same thing. Tell your children how Jesus has made a difference in your life. Explain to them how you came to Christ in the first place. Talk to them about answered prayer and give them examples from your life. Talk about salvation, forgiveness, and the difference Jesus can make in their lives. All of this is a living out of Deut. 11 in the context of Christianity.

It is also important to rehearse the details of Jesus' life again and again for your children, especially those dealing with His death, burial, and resurrection. I remember Pastor Dick Laue speaking at our church when my children were young and telling of how he talked and prayed with his kids every night; and he never let them go to sleep without reminding them that Jesus loved them enough to die for them on the cross, that He was buried, but that He arose again the third day and is alive right now. From that day forward I tried to regularly incorporate those elements, which make up the gospel, into bedtime with my kids.

From early on, long before they can read, I believe every child should have his or her own Bible, their Jesus Book. Reading age appropriate Bible stories from a Bible storybook is not only educational and faith building, but a wonderful time of bonding with your children as well. And praying with your kids is so important in cultivating faith. Teach your kids to talk to God as they would talk to their very best friend, for in reality that's who He is. Help them understand that God is all caring and wants to hear about all their thoughts and fears as well as their dreams. Make it clear that you don't have to use special, impressive-sounding words to talk to God, that just being honest and natural with Him is what He really wants.

When you are teaching your kids to pray it is important to help them realize that God doesn't always respond in just the way we expect, but that He does always respond. As a little boy I listened to the local college basketball team religiously. I never missed Vern Hawkins' play-by-play of the Southwest Missouri State Bears on KWTO. I had a couple of players that were my heroes and even wrote to them and got letters and pictures in return. I was as much a fan as an eight- or nine-year-old boy could possibly be. So it was natural that when they reached the NAIA championship game I would pray for them. I remember listening to the game and telling my mother I was confident that they would win because I had prayed that they would do so. My mother brought a dose of reality to my prayer life, however, when she reminded me that there might very well be another little boy in another city who was praying for the other team to win.

That night I learned a lot about prayer, including the fact that God doesn't always say yes to our prayers. Sometimes He says no or maybe or wait or He's got something even better for us. But through it all, my mother taught me that God would love me, and when things didn't go as I wanted, He would comfort me and He always wanted the best for me.

It is also important to talk about eternal life. Many people are in denial about death, and yet the Bible makes it clear that it is coming for all of us. The Bible also makes it clear that for the Christian, death is not a tragedy, instead it is going home. Children should not be sheltered from the reality of death. Instead, death should be a wonderful teaching opportunity about how we need to be prepared to die and that in Christ we can go to heaven. It is amazing to me how we have insulated ourselves from exposure to death. Even half a century ago, people most often died at home. Today it is most often in a hospital or hospice. A hundred years ago the body of the deceased often was prepared in the home and the visitation was held there as well. But today many children are totally sheltered from death. We've actually had ministry interns in our church who attended their first funeral only while interning with us. Let your children know that death is a reality and encourage them to live in such a way as to make every day count.

I've mentioned a number of things that cultivate faith. There are many other ways to help ground your family in the Christian faith as a basis for their making a commitment to a life in Christ. An interesting article in *The Lookout* magazine by Diane Brandmeyer listed fifteen ways to bring Jesus into your child's world.[3] Among her suggestions, at dinner ask, "What happened at school today that you can thank Jesus for?" She also suggests playing Christian tapes or CDs as you travel. Another idea was to put a note in your child's lunch that says, "Jesus and I think you are special because..." and finish the thought. Diane lists twelve more. But the number is limited only by your creativity and ingenuity.

YOUR CHILD'S NEED FOR CHRIST

There are all sorts of benefits to raising your children in a Christian home. Cultivating faith, raising your children in the church, praying and studying God's Word with them, these would all be good things even if there were no heaven or hell, no day of judgment, and this life was all there was. The Christian life is the greatest life one can live. But the fact is that there is a day of judgment, there is a heaven and there is a hell, and eternity is forever. So while it is important to teach your children the values and morals associated with the Christian life, and while it is important to provide for your children's physical, emotional, social, and material needs, what your children need more than anything else is a saving relationship with Jesus Christ.

Jesus said to Nicodemus, "Humans can reproduce only human life, but the Holy Spirit gives new life from heaven. So don't be surprised at my statement that you must be born again. Just as you can hear the wind but can't tell where it comes from or where it is going, so you can't explain how people are born of the Spirit" (John 3:6-7). Your top job as a parent is to be an evangelist in your own home, teaching your children their need for a Savior and pointing them to Jesus Christ as the only One who can save them.

Salvation is not something you can accomplish for your children. If you force, coerce, or manipulate your kids, you may very well pressure them into a false profession, which will stand in the way of genuine commitment later on in life. But you do have the responsibility to make sure they are not only exposed to but also taught the truth about salvation in Christ. Indeed, Paul writes in Rom. 10:14, "But how can they call on Him to save them unless they believe in Him? And how can they believe in Him if they have never heard about Him? And how can they hear about Him unless someone tells them?" And parent, you are their first and primary "someone."

LEADING YOUR CHILD TO CHRIST

What's the best approach to take? When should you begin teaching a child the need for salvation? How old is old enough for a child to come to Christ? The fact is that leading your child to Christ is a long-term, progressive effort that encompasses all of what we've talked about in this chapter. It begins at birth and continues until a child comes to what is sometimes called "the age of accountability." This is the age when a child knows right from wrong, understands that sin is disobedience to God, and is capable of being convicted of his or her personal sin. The specific age a child understands all that will differ from child to child based on background, personality, temperament, exposure to the truth, and many other factors.

Until children reach that level of awareness, parents should teach children to love the Lord but should certainly not encourage them to make a commitment to Christ. People cannot be saved until they know they're lost. People cannot repent unless they are aware of their sin. So for me, in working with children, that is the key factor in determining whether or not a child is ready to accept Christ as Savior. In my lengthy ministry I have heard many children make professions of faith based on the fact that they love Jesus. I've seen children baptized on the basis of their desire to obey God. At the time I'm writing this chapter my grandsons, Jack and Will, are only two and four years old. Yet I'll guarantee you that they love Jesus and that they want to obey God. But neither of those things has anything to do with their need for salvation or their readiness for salvation.

A raised hand at a revival, a prayer led by Mom while the child is sitting on her lap, a bedtime prayer asking Jesus into a child's heart, a child baptized without repentance from sin, are all sometimes assumed—depending upon theological background—to correspond to being born again, and excited parents often offer verbal assurances of salvation. Tragically, I believe there are many unregenerate people in the church who believe they are genuine Christians because they "did" something as a child.

But when children are old enough to inquire about becoming a Christian, they are old enough to be taught about becoming a Christian. And while it is not within the scope of this book to give you a verbatim of how I approach children, there are certain elements that need to be covered. The first of those elements is to establish the child's need for Christ. That comes from teaching on what sin is and determining if the child has an awareness of and guilt for sin. If not, there's really no use in going further. But if there is, a child should be taught the consequences of sin, which is ultimately eternal separation from God or hell itself.

Children should be made to know that Jesus Christ, God's Son, paid the price for us when He died on the cross, not for His own sins but for ours. He became our substitute, and most children understand the concept of a substitute as one who stands in for another. Then you should help the child understand that what Jesus did He did as a gift. Salvation is free for the taking. But we still have to accept it. Hundreds of times I've asked children, "If someone bought you a gift and really wanted you to have it and offered it to you, what would you still have to do before the gift would do you any good?" Nine times out of ten, kids will respond, "Say 'Thank you?'" At least most parents have taught their kids well in that regard.

While assuring children that they certainly should say, "Thank you," I also point out that what they really have to do is to receive or accept the gift. At that point children need to be taught how to accept the gift. They must be taught that we must believe that Jesus truly is the Son of God who died on the cross for our sins and was raised again; and that if we accept Him as Savior and Lord He will forgive us and save us. They must be taught about repentance for sin that not only means we are sorry but that we forsake that sin. And they must be taught that such belief and repentance are to be expressed in confession and Christian baptism.

Even if a child has an awareness of sin, I never push a young child for a decision. I review the basics of the gospel and will even ask if that's what he or she wants to do, to accept Jesus as Savior and be baptized into Him. But if a decision is to be made at that time it is because the child initiates it. For you as a parent or me as a pastor to push young children to commit their lives to Christ is to bring pressure to bear in which it will be next to impossible to determine if children are responding to Christ or responding to you. Believe me, I have no such reservations with teens or adults. But if the child is ready we should be more than happy to receive their confession of faith, pray with them, and make plans for their public confession and baptism. Some people are reluctant to baptize young children but not at all reluctant to receive their confession of faith or pray with them. Such a stance is impossible to defend biblically. If a child is too young to be baptized, he or she is too young to come to Christ in the first place.

A very simple but profound thing that I urge parents of young children to do when those young children come to Christ is to have them write out or dictate—if the child is unable to write out a testimony—of what they believe about Jesus and why they want to be baptized. The reason is that most children who come to Christ at an early age will later have doubts about their salvation based on the belief that they couldn't possibly have known what they were doing at seven or eight years old. When the parent takes out that written testimony that they've kept with the child's baptismal certificate during those intervening years, the now teenager will often be amazed at the depth of understanding they had at that early age.

IN CONCLUSION

Make sure your whole family is well-grounded in the Christian faith. Model a Christ-centered life. Teach your children about God. Read the Bible with them, to them, and for them. Make sure they understand the truth about the death, burial, and resurrection of Christ. Take your kids to church. See to it that they attend Bible School and youth group. And when they come to that age of accountability, lead them to accept Christ as personal Lord and Savior. If you feel totally inadequate, enlist the help of your pastor or youth pastor. For nothing is more important than seeing our kids come to Christ. And nothing brings more joy to the heart of a Christian parent than knowing that we are all saved.

Chapter Eleven

Respond to Rebellion

For many Christian parents, it is the ultimate horror story. Their child has turned away from the faith, rejected their values, and is choosing to live a life that is spiritually destructive and perhaps physically destructive as well. Such has been the cause of many a sleepless night and anxiety-filled day. Some parents even feel betrayed by God because they've tried to be good Christian parents and their kids have not turned out the way they had planned.

Of course, this problem is not peculiar to modern times. The Old Testament is filled with stories of children who betrayed their families' spiritual values. People like Hophni and Phinehas, sons of Eli the High Priest, or Absalom, son of King David. But the ultimate story of the rejection of family values is the story Jesus told of the Prodigal Son. No greater short story has ever been told in all of literature, scriptural or non-scriptural. It's the story of the boy who rejected his father, squandered his inheritance, and ended up in the pigpen.

Here's the story from the lips of Jesus as recorded in Luke 15:11-32 in the *New Living Translation:*

A man had two sons. The younger son told his father, "I want my share of your estate now, instead of waiting until you die. So his father agreed to divide his wealth between his sons. A few days later this younger son packed all his belongings and took a trip to a distant land, and there he wasted all his money on wild living. About the time his money ran out, a great famine swept over the land, and he began to starve. He persuaded a local farmer to hire him to feed his pigs. The boy became so hungry that even the pods he was feeding the pigs looked good to him. But no one gave him anything. When he finally came to his senses, he said to himself, "At home even the hired men have food enough to spare, and here I am, dying of hunger! I will go home to my father and say, 'Father, I have sinned against both heaven and you, and I am no longer worthy of being called your son. Please take me on as a hired man.'" So he returned home to his father. And while he was still a long distance away, his father saw him coming. Filled with love and compassion, he ran to his son, embraced him, and kissed him. His son said to him, "Father, I have sinned against both heaven and you, and I am no longer worthy of being called your son." But his father said to the servants, "Quick! Bring the finest robe in the house and put it on him. Get a ring for his finger, and sandals for his feet. And kill the calf we have been fattening in the pen. We must celebrate with a feast, for this son of mine was dead and has now returned to life. He was lost, but now he is found." So the party began. Meanwhile, the older son was in the fields working. When he returned home, he heard music and dancing in the house, and he asked one of the servants what was going on. "Your brother is back," he was told, "and your father has killed the calf we were fattening and has prepared a great feast. We are celebrating because of his safe return." The older brother was angry and wouldn't go in. His father came out and begged him, but he replied, "All these years I've worked hard for you and never once refused to do a single thing you told me to. And in all that time you never gave me even one young goat for a feast with my friends. Yet when this son of yours comes back after squandering your money on prostitutes, you celebrate by killing the finest calf we have. His father said to him, "Look, dear son, you and I are very close, and everything I have is yours. We had to celebrate this happy day. For your brother was dead and has come back to life! He was lost, but now he is found!"

Now, in that story we find some wise counsel on dealing with wayward children, and we'll look at some of those lessons before we close this chapter. The story gives us reason for hope and optimism. However, let me caution that neither this story nor any other passage of scripture gives any absolute guarantees. Children, even those raised in godly homes, sometimes reject the ethical values of their parents, adopt unbiblical beliefs, and take up worldly values and harmful lifestyles. And while there are actions we can take and attitudes we can have that make it more likely that the prodigal will come home, ultimately that child must exercise his or her free will in returning to the righteous values they once rejected. Indeed, there are those who walk or run away from their upbringing, never to return.

Many times over the years I have had parents tell me they are angry with God because they raised their kids right, prayed for them through years of waywardness, and yet they see no positive results. They somehow feel that God has not done His part. But man was not created as a puppet with his strings being pulled by the heavenly puppeteer. Man has been given free will that can be used for his good or for his detriment, for his success or for self-imposed defeat. However, there are principles we can follow that will greatly enhance the likelihood of a wayward child "coming to his senses," and returning home.

This is a broad topic. We could be talking about a junior high student arguing about going to church or a high school student getting in with the wrong crowd or a recent graduate refusing to live by the house rules. We could be talking about a college student coming home to announce that he no longer believes in God. Specifics about various facets of rebelliousness would take far more space than we have, but hopefully the general principles covered will be helpful, and the Holy Spirit will help you make the specific application.

REBELLION

As noted above, rebellion takes many different forms. Let's at least identify some of the more egregious ways children of believers rebel.

First, there is a rejection of your *moral code*. Who you are is largely expressed by what you believe about right and wrong behavior. Your identity is also expressed by the way you actually behave. Thus, when your kids reject your moral code, you feel they have rejected you. The same is true with your *lifestyle*. Most parents provide a certain standard of living, a certain level of education, a certain preference in friends, as well as their moral code. Again, when a child chooses to reject that lifestyle, the parent may feel rejected. But notice the difference. Your moral code, if it is based upon God's Word should be an absolute, while lifestyle is a matter of personal choice. Rejection of either may be painful for you as a parent. However, the former is of far greater significance and should be a cause for far greater concern.

The same could be said of the rejection of your *church*. I believe that church attendance at the church of the parents' choice should not be optional in the younger years, and church attendance itself should not be optional as long as a child is living at home. However, we all have personal preferences, and there is a significant difference between not wanting to attend a certain church and not wanting to attend church at all. Our church at Kingsway tends to be a very family oriented church. We have a number of young adults who have grown up in the church who now worship at Common Ground Christian Church, a young adult oriented congregation in Broad Ripple. They go there not in rejection of the church of their parents but in search of a broader fellowship of young adults and a more edgy approach to worship. As they get married they tend to find their way back.

Contrast that, however, with the rejection of the parents' *faith*, if it is a Biblical faith, and we're talking about something of great consequence. Sometimes the rejection of morals, lifestyle, and church is a progression leading to a rejection of God. Sometimes God and faith are identified with Christian parents when a young person rebels against his or her parents, and the young person ends up rebelling against God as well.

In an earlier chapter we explored the rebellion associated with substance abuse. Then there are the issues of promiscuity and its likely companion, pregnancy. Even Christian homes have had to deal with issues of teen prostitution. Today's promotion of the gay agenda provides an added temptation for kids to experiment with homosexuality and lesbianism. Hate groups proliferate. And of course, there's the ongoing appeal of cults that thrive on the university and college campuses.

I say all that to put things in proper perspective. I have dealt with parents devastated by all these issues. I have ministered to prodigals who have run away to all these "distant lands." But the rebelliousness most parents have to confront does not approach these levels. Much of it has to do with rebellion toward issues like curfew, honesty, grades at school, required chores at home, use of the car, dating rules, dress code, and involvement in certain youth programs at church. However, the same basic principles for how to deal with rebellion apply whether we're dealing with issues of relatively minor consequence or the most significant of issues.

RESTRICTIONS

Before we get into the specific responses to rebellion, let's review some of the areas of control parents have in influencing children's behavior. These are restrictions that need to be maintained and used wisely.

We can't always control our children's behavior outside of our presence, but we can certainly refuse to provide the *finances* to do that which is contrary to our wishes. We can't force our children to adopt our *family values*, but we can insist they live by them as long as they live in our home. We can't impose our *faith* upon our children, but we can insist that it be adhered to and honored by each member of our family.

Because these issues were all dealt with in detail in earlier chapters, I won't repeat myself now, but *discipline, communication,* and *time* are three other areas over which we as parents have control. We can insist upon the restrictions implied by each one. Not only do we have the right to use finances, family values, faith, discipline, communication, and time to control rebellion on the part of our kids, we also have the God given responsibility to do so. When that rebellious, 18-year-old son says, "I can do whatever I want to do; you have no authority over me," it is time to say, "You are absolutely right. But you cannot and will not do it in my home. And if you can't respect that, then it is time for you to move out on your own."

RESPONSE

Let me give you nine specific responses to rebellion in our kids. Again, the specific application will vary from age to age and degree of seriousness. But all of these responses are applicable across the board.

Practice Unconditional Love

Actually, God's unconditional love for us is the central theme of the parable of the prodigal son. Look at the father's response to the son's request for his part of the inheritance, which he had no right to claim until his father's death. His dad granted him his request. A child is born into our care by God's providence, and it is important that we love that child, love him or her unconditionally, as God loves us.

Unconditional love is a matter of choice. It is an action, a decision, an attitude of the heart that must be based on God's love for us and is renewed each day of our lives, regardless of what our children have done. Our relationship with our children is not based on their actions, but on God's unconditional love, which we in turn share with our children. So the first principle of response is to develop a parenting strategy that is based on the solid foundation of unconditional love. However, unconditional love does not mean we condone the rebellion or the sin. It simply means that we *focus on the person, not the sin.*

Every parent should try to maintain a relationship with his or her child, focusing on the child's entire life and not just the area of conflict. To focus only on the sin or rebellion will most certainly lead to tension and alienation. But when parents keep their concern for their son or daughter foremost in their minds, they can still communicate unconditional love without in any way implying approval of the sin. That does not mean that the parent financially supports their child's irresponsible behavior or tolerates it in their home. It does mean they neither reject nor stop loving their child just because they are in rebellion.

Network with Other Christians

One of the blessings of being a part of a Bible-believing, Christ-honoring congregation of believers is that we can help one another, even in dealing with wayward children. I believe we need to see our families as part of the larger community of God's people. We need to recognize potential helpers within the family who are gifted in relating to our kids. This is no time for pride. If someone else can get through to my kids when I can't, I should be more than happy to invite their involvement.

If a young person struggles with questions about his or her faith, it may be time for him or her to sit down and talk with the pastor or youth pastor. Behavioral problems might mean it's time to see a Christian counselor. But there are lay people in the church who have either struggled with your children's struggles or helped their own children through those same struggles. Be discerning and discreet, but involve other members of your spiritual family in helping your kids through the tough challenges they face.

Reaffirm the Rules

In the chapter on discipline we discussed guidelines for determining the house rules. When kids are challenging those rules it is time to reaffirm them and remove any ambiguity about exactly what they mean. Our children need to understand that as long as they are living at home, the parents will establish the standards of behavior. Sometimes rebellious behavior will require the introduction of new rules to deal with that specific, but unanticipated behavior.

Dedicate Adequate Time

Make yourself available to your prodigal. Arrange for nonthreatening time together to reopen the lines of communication. If possible, schedule a special trip for some enjoyable one-on-one time.

Remember to Listen

Tragically, many instances of rebellion only polarize parents and their prodigal. Planned conversations turn into shouting matches. Let it go. Especially in extreme cases, the child already knows his or her behavior is unacceptable. You don't have to tell the child again and again. Instead, work on breaking down the wall of hostility or indifference your child may have built around himself or herself, and have meaningful conversations. Again, that means listening at least as much and preferably more than you speak.

Refuse to Argue

Many times a rebellious son or daughter will try to drag you into an argument about whether a choice he or she has made is right or wrong. Rarely is this a search for the truth. Most kids already know what's right and what's wrong. However, they do want to get you on the defensive. They do want to make you lose your cool. There is certainly a time for rational discussion about life choices. However, when the exchange becomes defensive and starts to heat up, it is time to back off and refuse to be dragged into an argument.

Don't Panic

I know I've said it several times in one way or another, but it is so important that parents not overreact. What if your child becomes openly rebellious or even engages in illegal or immoral behavior? Again, the first rule is, don't panic. There are limits to your control. There are only certain restrictions you can enforce. So stay calm, rational, do your best, follow the principles of this chapter, and turn it all over to the Lord. All of which brings us to the last principle.

Pray Fervently

Prayer is in many ways the easiest principle for us to practice. Yet many parents do not pray as they should because prayer calls on us to recognize that we are not sufficient to meet the needs of our children without divine help. It is both humbling and a little frightening to recognize that we need God to act in our child's heart for any of our efforts to have the desired, long-term effect. There are many things you cannot do in response to your child's rebellion; but you can *always* pray. And I've witnessed the prayers of godly fathers and mothers rescue their children from outrageous rebellion and destructive behavior of every type.

One of the most powerful testimonies I've ever heard in this regard has to do with the daughter of Jim Cymbala, pastor of Brooklyn Tabernacle Church in New York City. Though raised by godly parents in a wonderful church, she rebelled as a teen and got involved in a life of drugs and depravity and began selling her body to support her habits. She was gone from home for years without even contacting her parents. Jim and Carol never stopped praying for her. Then during one Tuesday night prayer service, a lady in the congregation urged Pastor Cymbala to focus that night on prayer for his daughter.

You can read the whole story in Cymbala's book, *Fresh Wind, Fresh Fire*,[1] but it was later that week that his daughter showed up at their front door, having traveled all the way from California, pulled by the fact that she knew people were praying for her. Today, a godly woman, a pastor's wife with a great ministry, she is also a great testimony to the power of prayer in reaching the prodigal.

THE GRACE CONNECTION

The parable of the prodigal son is a remarkable teaching on many themes. But if there is one concept that permeates the whole story it is the concept of *grace*. Dr. Dan Allender, in his excellent book, *How Children Raise Parents*,[2] points out three functions of grace that we all desperately need. Let me close by focusing on those three functions.

Grace Waits

The Father in the story waited patiently for his son to return. We can imagine him on the front porch of the family home, scanning the horizon, his hand shading his eyes, squinting, hopeful of getting a glimpse of his returning son. How many days, weeks, months, or years did he wait? I don't think it was by chance that the father saw the son returning. He was looking for him. Others might have given up hope, but not this father.

And while the father in the parable represents God, it is God who gives us the ultimate expression of how grace waits.

Grace Runs

There is only one passage in the entire Bible where God is pictured as getting in a hurry. When the father sees the son approaching, he can't contain himself. He doesn't worry about his age, conditioning, or decorum. He is thrilled beyond words that his son who was gone has returned. Now, quite honestly, most fathers of that day would not have accepted a disgraced son home, let alone run to meet him. But remember, this father is a picture of God. And we see in him the total abandon of joy unbound. People who know joy can't sit still. They run, leap, twirl, and dance. The son, whom the father feared was dead, was alive! It was time to run.

Grace Parties

There are parties that are planned. The guest list is refined again and again, the menu is carefully thought through, the decorations and music have to be just right. But this is a spontaneous celebration. There were two things that characterized it more than anything else. There was the joy of the father upon the return of the son. And there was the grace experienced by the son at the expense of the father. But this is a celebration of life. The son was dead and is alive again. Grace has to throw a party.

Of course, there is another element to the story that we've not explored—that of the elder son, the faithful, obedient child who never rebels. But that's another subject for another time. Praise God, there are success stories, there are prodigals that come home, and there are rebels who repent. Let's celebrate that and practice the principles that are used of God in bringing it about.

Chapter Twelve

Ascribe Value

I realize some people will dismiss the content of this book as being out of touch with child rearing in this challenging new day in which we live. I readily acknowledge that times are getting tougher and the challenges of parenting are getting greater. I've already confessed my wish that every kid could grow up as I did in the wonderful days of the fifties. Those were the days when Dick and Mac McDonald started a hamburger chain that now stretches around the world. Those were the days when cars got bigger every year and grew fins as well. Those were the days when Holiday Inns began to dot the roads of America. That was the innocent era of "I Love Lucy."

In those days, "Leave It to Beaver," "The Adventures of Ozzie and Harriet," and "Father Knows Best" were more than television shows, they were a way of life for millions of Americans. Oh, of course, there were significant problems. But there was a low divorce rate. A higher percentage of people attended church than ever before or since. Entertainment was for the most part wholesome and free of the violence, profanity, and gratuitous sex, which is now more the rule than the exception. Each school day began with The Pledge of Allegiance and prayer, and the Bible still had a prominent place in the public school classroom. Drugs were all but nonexistent and teen alcoholism was all but unheard of.

What a contrast to our modern day world in which AIDS is the sixth leading cause of death for young people, 15 to 24 years of age.[1] Every ninety seconds a teenager attempts suicide somewhere in America. We live in a world where six out of ten children will live in a single-parent home; one in twenty are raised by grandparents; and one third of children do no live with their biological father. The deterioration of society as a whole makes it more challenging than ever to raise "G-Rated" kids.

Furthermore, even in better times, parents who have worked hard at being good parents have not always been successful. One such parent wrote, "I've been as good a parent as I could possibly be, I think. We've been a very close family. We've done everything we could do according to the book, such as taken vacations together, gone on backpack trips together, traveled extensively all over the world. We've been a good Christian family. My wife and I tried to set a good example by *being* a good example. We have tried to keep our children up to date on what dangerous things are, but perhaps we did not bear down as hard as we should."

Those words were written by Art Linkletter shortly after his daughter, Diane, age 20, took a hit of acid and jumped to her death out of the kitchen window of her sixth-floor Hollywood apartment. The Linkletters were not alone in their heartache. Thomas Edison's son, Thomas Jr., had a drinking problem and committed suicide. Three of Winston Churchill's children led very troubled lives. The great evangelist, Billy Sunday, reached hundreds of thousands for Christ but could not reach his own two sons. Oral Roberts' son, Ronnie, spent the last few months of his life high on drugs and alcohol and died of a self-inflicted gunshot wound to the heart. Conversely, atheist Madalyn Murray O'Hare's son, Bill, became a leading evangelical, even though his mother used him as the plaintiff in the Supreme Court case that resulted in Bible reading and prayer being removed from the public schools.

So let me acknowledge again that the times are getting tougher, and there are no absolute guarantees that your kids are going to be "G-Rated," regardless of what you do. However, following the eleven principles we've discussed thus far will greatly enhance the likelihood of your children growing up physically, mentally, socially, and spiritually healthy. However, there is a final principle that actually should permeate the practice of all the other principles. This is a practice that I believe to be absolutely essential to Biblically based, child-nurturing, Christ-honoring parenting. *Ascribing value* to our children should be part and parcel of every other principle I've advocated. There are three very specific ways in which we can do that.

Applaud Your Child's Uniqueness

We value consistency. We live in a franchise-oriented world. I can walk into a McDonald's anywhere in the world and know that I can order and receive pretty much the same thing I can get back home. The arches, the color scheme, and Ronald McDonald himself are all the same. A Big Mac in Avon, Indiana, is basically the same as the one I can order near Red Square in Moscow or just off Tiananmen Square in Beijing. When the new Super Wal-Mart opened near our home I walked in and said, "It seems like I've been here before."

But children aren't franchises or products. Each child is unique. So focus on and applaud each child's uniqueness. No matter how many children you may have, unless your first child is part of a multiple birth, he or she is an only child for a while. It is a real temptation to lavish attention on that child that is missing in the lives of your other children. Of course, there is also a tendency to give special attention to the baby of the family. Thus it is not unusual, as my wife, a middle child, often points out, for the middle kids to feel slighted, ignored, or forgotten. Every child has worth. Every child is important to God. Every child is unique and we need to celebrate and applaud that uniqueness.

Focus on Each Child

I can't overemphasize the importance of one-on-one times between a parent and each child. We've already discussed father-daughter dates and regularly scheduled father-son nights out. Spending time with each child communicates that he or she is an important individual and not just one of the kids. Obviously, the same principle applies to mothers and their children.

Help Them Identify Personal Gifts and Talents

One of the best ways to applaud your child's uniqueness is by assisting him or her in identifying and developing God given skills. And one of the best ways to do that is by encouraging him or her to be involved in different activities, and not necessarily the activities we as parents are most interested in. It is easy for a father who was a star football player to assume that his son is going to play football or for a mother who was an outstanding pianist to push her daughter toward playing the piano. However, children should be encouraged to explore a variety of options.

Some activities will soon be discarded. That doesn't mean the initial pursuit was a waste of time or money, it was simply a part of the process of discovery. Jennifer played soccer as a first grader. However, most of her time on the field was spent picking dandelions or watching butterflies. She did score a goal—when someone else kicked the ball and it caromed off of her into the net. However, it was easy to see that Mia Hamm she wasn't. Piano lessons were of much greater interest. And while she did not become an accomplished pianist, that pursuit gave her many hours of enjoyment and a skill that she still enjoys today. She did, however, become quite an accomplished flutist, with significant accomplishments in both band and music contest competition.

So look for your child's strengths, interests, and natural abilities and encourage the pursuit of those things. Some children will be strong in academics. Some may have a special affinity for scouting programs or drama. Others may really get into art, photography, or computers. Encourage your kids to develop the skills in which they are most interested. Kids need to feel competent in at least some area of their life. That's why junior high students seem to try out for everything such as sports, music, drama, student government; you name it. They are trying to find that special niche, that unique place of belonging.

Whatever areas of involvement your children choose, be their biggest cheerleader. There has never been a youth baseball, football, or basketball game played where each competitor did not look into the stands to see if his or her parents where there and where they were seated.

There has never been a band concert, an awards ceremony, or school play where it was insignificant to the child that Mom and Dad were there. And when parents choose to neglect to cheer their child on, it leaves wounds that are next too impossible to heal.

Whatever you do, don't abdicate your role as chief cheerleader. You are given the unparalleled opportunity of discerning your child's unique gifts, talents, interests, and personality. Use the things you learn in both identifying and affirming that uniqueness. I'm not talking about mis-guided compliments or insincere flattery. I am talking about discovering, affirming, and applauding your child's uniqueness. Recognize that each child is "fearfully and wonderfully made."

Help Them Achieve their Goals

Having once identified your child's uniqueness, you can also help them deal with the challenges they face in becoming all they are intended to be. No, you can't do it for them, but you can be an enabler—a fa-cilitator. When they fall down, you can be there to help them get back up. Your children have dreams, but they don't have experience, and they probably don't have the know-how to understand the importance of goals and to understand the process of accomplishing those goals. Just make sure they are their goals, not yours. And when they succeed, be there to applaud them. When they fail, be there to applaud them as special people just the same. Encourage them to do their best. But remember that perfection has eluded every person who ever walked this earth except for One.

Affirm Your Child's Worth

Fred Hartley, in his book, *Parenting at Its Best*, gives numerous words of affirmation for a parent to offer his or her child. Because some of us struggle in this area, let me list a few of those affirming statements Hartley mentions:[2]

> "I love you for who you are right now, not just for who you will become."
> "I like you just the way you are, not for who I can make you be."
> "I embrace you for one simple, overarching reason—you are you and nobody else."
> "You are one-of-a-kind, unique, special, significant."
> "You are not perfect, but you are perfect for me."

"I love you not because of what you do but simply because you are my son/daughter."

"I will love you if you pass or fail."

"You are you and I'd lay down my life to defend your right to be the unique person you are."

"You are without question one of the choicest gifts God has ever given me."

"I like the way God made you."

"You are unique."

"I admire you."

"You are a winner."

"I love watching you become your own person."

"There is no one else who could ever take your place."

All children long for such affirmation. They want to know that they are accepted for who they are and that you affirm their worth. We've already made it clear that parenting is much more than mere affirmation. We've also made it clear that there are certain things your child may do that you not only don't affirm, you condemn. But there is a world of difference between condemning the act and condemning the child. And when your child already knows that you value them as a person and love them unconditionally, they can accept your condemnation of their actions constructively rather than as an assault against them.

Your kids are going to get beat up at school, not literally, although that might happen too. They are going to sometimes feel devalued by their friends. But if Mom and Dad are there as a safety net, affirming their worth, applauding their uniqueness, then they can make it through those other assaults that are sure to come.

Accept Your Child's Identity

Applause and affirmation are both important to a child. However, they will probably be viewed as insincere at best if they are not accompanied by acceptance. Affirmation without acceptance leaves a child feeling that he or she still needs to perform, measure up, and earn his or her parents' favor. But when a child feels his or her parents' acceptance, then those words of affirmation only allow the child to feel better and better about himself or herself.

Jan and I are thoroughly enjoying the parenting being done by our son and our daughter-in-law. Shan and Lise are great parents. We both see them as far better parents than we ever were. But Jack and Will obviously know they are valued, accepted, loved unconditionally, and thus are constantly affirmed as well. You can tell it from the happiness that radiates from their lives.

You never hear a conversation at their house without hearing the words, "Good job, Jack!" "Good job, Will!" You also hear, "You're such a helper. I'm so proud of you. God made you so special. You are such a good boy!" And kids thrive on such acceptance and affirmation.

Dr. John Trent tells a story that was related to him at one of his conferences. It was the story of a father taking his toddler-aged daughter out for breakfast. They had just gotten their pancakes when the dad decided it would be a good time to tell his daughter how much he loved and appreciated her. "Jenny," the dad said, "I want you to know how much I love you, and how special you are to Mom and me. We prayed for you for years, and now that you're here and growing up to be such a wonderful girl, we couldn't be more proud of you."

Once he had said all that, he stopped talking and reached for his fork to start eating. But before he could do so his daughter reached her little hand out, laid it on her father's hand, and with a soft, pleading voice she said, "Longer, Daddy, longer." He put his fork back down and proceeded to tell her some more of the reasons he loved and appreciated her. Again, he started to eat, but a second, third, and fourth time he heard her say, "Longer, Daddy, longer." His pancakes may have gotten cold, but a little girl got the emotional nourishment she needed that day.

Affirming, accepting words have such power. Over the years I've asked many preachers why they went into the ministry. A disproportionate number have mentioned someone they respected, early in life, saying, "You know, I think God just might want to use you as a preacher someday." The wise man was right, "Everyone enjoys a fitting reply; it is wonderful to say the right thing at the right time" (Prov. 15:23).

Let me urge you to look for ways to affirm and praise your children every day. Even the most difficult of days yields some nugget worthy of praise if you're looking for it. Bedtime is a good time to review your day, and if there has been no applause, affirmation, or acceptance expressed, make sure the situation is corrected. And be specific with your praise. Just the other day we were at our son's and daughter-in-law's house and Lise was babysitting two other children in addition to her own two. Jack picked up a toy and took it over to the little girl and offered it to her. Right away his mommy said, "Jack, I really like the way you share your toys with Allie. That makes me very happy."

Children grow up awfully fast. Don't miss those daily opportunities to applaud, affirm, and accept. Those words of encouragement and affirmation are like seeds that will sprout forth with a wonderful harvest of good things in the lives of our kids.

Ephesians 4:29 has a much broader application than parenting, but parenting is certainly included: "Don't use foul or abusive language. Let everything you say be good and helpful, so that your words will be an encouragement to those who hear them." And don't miss Paul's words in Eph. 5:15-16, "So be careful how you live, not as fools but as those who are wise. Make the most of every opportunity for doing good in these evil days."

What We Did Right

Over a decade ago when Shan was still in college and Jennifer in high school, I was teaching a class on parenting, and I asked both of them to make a list of things they felt Jan and I did right as parents. They didn't collaborate on their lists. And both of them included a few things that were tongue-in-cheek. Their lists not only will give you some insights into our home, but will remind you of many of the things that are important for your kids as well.

Shan's List:
1. They inspired a sincere love for the Indiana Hoosiers and St. Louis Cardinals.
2. They showed real interest in everything I did, even after I left home.
3. They cared about my friend's lives.
4. They taught me respect for authority, other's feelings, money, and enforced this respect (i.e. "Woody" the spoon).
5. They liked me, and didn't just love me. Then they told me so.

6. They allowed me complete freedom as long as I practiced responsibility with that freedom.
7. They never laid huge expectations on me but encouraged me to get involved socially, educationally, politically, etc.
8. They let me fail and fall on my face, but not too often.
9. They made themselves role models of Christian people and a Christian couple.
10. They left every parting so that the next meeting could be in heaven without regret.
11. They taught me the importance of being in church even when the World Series or Super Bowl was on.
12. They showed me and then allowed me to find for myself the meaning of this life.

Jennifer's List:
1. They always told me how much they loved me, encouraged me, and complimented me.
2. They were strict. That showed how much they really cared.
3. They didn't give me everything I wanted.
4. They taught me about Jesus and the Bible.
5. They showed me the importance of "family time" such as vacations, Thursday night dates, etc.
6. They gave me advice, but let me make my own decisions.
7. They taught me the importance of communication.
8. They were interested in my life and my feelings.
9. They were never too busy to listen.
10. They sent me to a Christian school.
11. They made sure all my friends were decent.
12. They taught me respect and manners.
13. They always tried to understand.
14. They always attended my performances or anything else really important to me.
15. They taught me to love the Hoosiers, Cardinals, and Disney.
16. They helped me gain morals and standards and showed me what to look for in a husband.

The fact is, just about the time we felt we were learning how to be good parents, it came time to begin the process of "de-parenting," which in many respects is more difficult than parenting. But just as eaglets are not intended to stay in the nest, so part of the goal of parenting is to prepare our children to live independent lives. However, that process actually begins when we first become parents and continues for the rest of our lives. For the act of birth is, in a sense, an act of parental release. So is placing the baby in his or her own bed, weaning, leaving that baby for the first time with a babysitter, putting him or her in preschool, letting go of the bike, watching him or her ride away on the school bus, that first overnighter at a friend's house, giving him or her the keys to the car, and taking him or her away to college. Each of these steps says in ways big or small, "I believe in you. You are unique. You are special. You are your own person. I trust you. I love you!"

One book I read compares de-parenting as part of a relay race. Our parents passed the baton off to us, and it is ours to pass off to our children. Rather than measured in yards or miles, this race is measured in generations. And as difficult and painful as it sometimes may be, it should be our goal to pass the baton well.

To me, the passing of the baton was best symbolized in the weddings of our children. I had the high responsibility and unspeakable privilege of officiating at both Shan and Jennifer's weddings. The dual responsibilities of father of the bride and officiating pastor were almost too much for me on Jennifer's wedding day, especially given the fact that I lost the wedding license. Even so, I thought I was pretty well under control until the processional was underway, and I was standing in the foyer with this beautiful young woman, arm in arm, and she said, "Daddy, can we pray together?" And all the memories came flooding back in a torrent, 25 years compacted into a few seconds, and the significance of what was taking place really hit me.

Shan has always had many close friends. So I was both surprised and more honored than you can imagine when he asked me not only to co-officiate with Lise's pastor, Wally Rendel, at their wedding, but to serve as his best man as well. We were both standing at the front of the church in Lexington, Kentucky, all decked out in our rented tuxes. Shan had already earned three degrees; he had been living on his own

Endnotes

Chapter 1

1. Jerry Johnston, *How to Save Your Kids from Ruin* (Wheaton, Ill.: Victor Books, 1994), 89.
2. Gary D. Chapman, *The Five Love Languages of Children* (New Man Magazine, March/April, 1998), 38.
3. Joel Smith, *How to Have the Children of Your Dreams* (Sermon preached at Wellspring Community Church, June 17, 2001), 2.
4. Chuck Lancock and Dave Veerman, *From Dad with Love* (Wheaton, Ill.: Tyndale House, 1994), 121.

Chapter 2

1. Ross Campbell, *How to Really Love Your Child* (Wheaton, Ill.: Victor Books, 1979), 56.
2. Quentin J. Schultze, *Winning Your Kids Back from the Media* (Downers Grove, Ill.: InterVarsity Press, 1994), 31.

Chapter 3

1. Robert and Debra Bruce, *Reclaiming Your Family* (Nashville: Broadman and Holman, 1994), 157.
2. Kathi Hunter, "Connect with Your Kids" (*Christian Parenting Today*, August 5, 2003), 1.
3. Laura Schlessinger, *Ten Stupid Things Men Do to Mess Up Their Lives* (New York: Harper Collins, 1997), 231.
4. Hunter, *Christian Parenting Today*, 1.
5. Schlessinger, *Ten Stupid Things Men Do to Mess Up Their Lives*, 230.
6. Bruce, *Reclaiming Your Family*, 181.

Chapter 4

1. Dan B. Allender, *How Children Raise Parents* (Colorado Springs: Waterbrook Press, 2003), 213.
2. Fred A. Hartlely III, *Parenting At Its Best* (Grand Rapids: Fleming H. Rwell, 2003), 103.

Chapter 5

1. Bruce, *Reclaiming Your Family*, 56-57.
2. *The Washington Times*, August 25, 2001, 1.
3. Jack Hyles, *How to Rear Children* (Hammond, In.: Hyle-Anderson, 1972), 93-96.
4. Rick Fowler, *The Ground Rules* (*Christian Parenting Today,* May/June 2002).
5. Ted Tripp, *Shepherding a Child's Heart* (Wapwallspen, Penn.: Shepherd Press, 2001), 150.

Chapter 6

1. Leman, Kevin, *Adolescence Isn't Terminal* (Wheaton, Ill.: Tyndale House, 2002), 75.
2. Ibid., 76.
3. A.W. Tozer, *Renewed Day by Day* (Harrisburg, Penn.: Christian Publication, 1980), 114.

4. Ritch Grimes, *Teach Your Children* (Sermon preached Sept. 23, 2003, SermonCentral.com.).
5. Leman, 79.
6. *Guidepost*, 1989, Quoted in Grimes sermon.
7. www.AnswersInGenesis.org
8. Josh McDowell, *Why True Love Waits* (Wheaton, Ill.: Tyndale House, 2002).
9. Gordon Dalbey, *Healing the Masculine Soul* (Dallas: Word, 1988), 174-175.
10. Hartley, 199.

Chapter 7

1. Leman, Kevin, 171.
2. Johnston, 158-164.
3. Donald W. Welch, *Parenting* (Fall 2003 e-mail).

Chapter 8

1. Bob Waliszewski, *Seven Keys to Media-Proofing Your Kids* (Indiana Family Institute, Issue #1, 2001), 1.
2. Quentin J. Schultze, *Winning Your Kids Back From the Media* (Downers Grove, Ill.: InterVarsity Press, 1994), 96.
3. Bruce, 230.
4. Schultze, 42.

Chapter 9

1. James Dobson, *The New Dare to Discipline* (Wheaton, Ill.: Tyndale House, 1992), 256.
2. Ted G. Stone and Philip D. Barber, *Victory Through Parenting* (*SBC Life*, January 2002), 12.

Chapter 10

1. John R. Westerhoff III, *Will Our Children Have Faith?* (Minneapolis: Seaburg Press, 1976).

2. Campbell, 18.
3. Diane Lesire Brandmeyer, *15 Ways to Bring Jesus Into Your Child's World* (*The Lookout*, November 16, 1995), 8.

Chapter 11

1. Jim Cymbala, *Fresh Wind, Fresh Fire* (Grand Rapids: Zondervan, 1997), 59-66.
2. Allender, 183-187.

Chapter 12

1. Johnston, 38.
2. Hartley, 64-66.

Pleasant Word

Printed in the United States
84768LV00004B/154-156/A